STARTING A NEW LIFE
IN RURAL AMERICA

WARNING

The information and procedures described in this book inevitably reflect the author's individual beliefs and experience under specific circumstances that the reader cannot duplicate exactly. The information in this book should therefore be considered for academic study only. Neither the author, publisher, or distributors of this book assume any responsibility for the use or misuse of information contained in this book.

STARTING A NEW LIFE
IN RURAL AMERICA

21 THINGS YOU NEED TO KNOW BEFORE YOU MAKE YOUR MOVE

RAGNAR BENSON

PALADIN PRESS ~ BOULDER, COLORADO

Other books by Ragnar Benson:
Acquiring New ID
Do-It-Yourself Medicine
Eating Cheap
Guerrilla Gunsmithing
Live Off the Land in the City and Country
Mantrapping
Modern Survival Retreat
Modern Weapons Caching
Ragnar's Action Encyclopedias, Volumes 1 and 2
Ragnar's Guide to Interviews, Investigations, and Interrogations
Ragnar's Guide to the Underground Economy
Ragnar's Tall Tales
Ragnar's Ten Best Traps . . . And a Few Others That Are Damn Good, Too
Ragnar's Urban Survival
Survivalist's Medicine Chest
The Survival Nurse
Survival Poaching
The Survival Retreat: A Total Plan for Retreat Defense

Starting a New Life in Rural America:
21 Things You Need to Know Before You Make Your Move
by Ragnar Benson

Copyright © 2006 by Ragnar Benson

ISBN 13: 978-1-58160-493-1
Printed in the United States of America

Published by Paladin Press, a division of
Paladin Enterprises, Inc.
Gunbarrel Tech Center, 7077 Winchester Circle
Boulder, Colorado 80301 USA, +1.303.443.7250

Direct inquiries and/or orders to the above address.

Visit our website at www.paladin-press.com

Contents

Preface

For most of the last 65 years, I have made my home out in the country. At times it was way, way out in the country. In the course of this more than six decades, I have had numerous opportunities to interact with suburban and city transplants in the country, enough to realize that their dream of establishing a remote island of nature around them can quickly and easily turn to worms, often with great trauma and financial pain. Good, honest, hard-working folks with a dream of a quiet life in the country do not always understand the essential progression of things in the sticks, nor how business is properly conducted in that social context. In the end, this prevents them from finding the adventure and peace of rural living for which they yearn.

My experience hasn't been completely limited to country living. For several brief periods I did live in the big city, once in a luxury condo with all the amenities. Very nice to drive into my own private parking spot in the basement and ride the elevator up to my pad overlooking the city. It was also nice not to have to worry about trimming trees, cutting fire breaks, mowing grass, dealing with marauding critters, handling septic stops and power outages, or even getting to the grocery store.

Did I like it? Yes, but I always knew that my stay in the city was temporary. Returning to my peaceful, picturesque place out on the mountain was always the future.

As a kid I spent at least half my time on an old-fashioned, rough-and-tumble family farm run by my grandparents. There was no heat in our bedrooms in winter, and opening the windows was the only air conditioning in the summer. I quickly learned about lightning rods, summer wash kitchens, destructive windstorms, droughts, bugs, rats, and being snowed in, not to mention sleeping in the hay mow, hauling water, cleaning the heat stove, and replenishing the cook stove kindling. Believe me, I am no more nostalgic for old family farms than I am for that city condo. Done correctly, country living is as good as it gets, but a working family farm wasn't it for me.

The point is, because I have lived both in the city and in the country, I often find myself cast in the role of counselor to suburban and city people moving to the country for the first time. Having done this for so many years, I thought it would be helpful to write a book that covers issues that are common knowledge to long-time rural residents but may be totally out of the realm of experience for others. Country life, even with the bumps and warts, really is fun, especially for those with some idea about what lies ahead. That's what this book is all about.

Introduction

Understanding how to live comfortably, efficiently, and happily in the country is best done with real-life examples. Experience is always a good teacher.

The following incident started with a call from an attorney in Washington State. Seems he had a seriously ill client who, having recently moved from the big city to her country dream house, was being seriously—perhaps fatally—threatened by the actions of her county highway department and the county commissioners. Both sides were heavily polarized. The attorney wanted to know if I would investigate and offer guidance in what already was an ugly situation.

The woman—an extremely wealthy lady with a serious asthmatic condition—moved out to the country believing pure rural air would be a benefit. She bought a newer existing home located 2 miles past the end of the blacktop on a dusty gravel road. Soil in that area was formed over volcanic rock and mica, an instant formula for choking clouds of dust. Fine micaceous dust from road traffic a scant 80 yards downwind from her home infiltrated her residence, creating a life-threatening situation. Her husband was terrified that her next gasp of air could be the lady's last.

Her explanation for such an obviously foolish move involved the fact that she firmly believed she had received a binding commitment from the county to run new blacktop out past her home.

On the one hand, there were indications that such a commitment had been made through a Realtor and one of three county commissioners, perhaps to both husband and wife. On the other hand, my conversations with county highway folks and the commissioners as a group convinced me that the asthmatic lady had absolutely no concept of how politics work in small rural communities. Under the circumstances, and due to her incessant hectoring, there wasn't going to be any additional blacktop. Doing the job with her own funds was easily possible, but she, by God, was going to teach those lying, stupid country bumpkins a lesson!

As it all unfolded, I thought to myself that many of the problems that newly moved city slickers encounter in the country were present in this situation. Her concept of the role of social values and responsibilities, community interaction, and even the place of a local church in community affairs was not only grossly misdirected, it was in total error.

For starters, the lady was not a member of any church. That's a personal choice, and that's fine, but she failed to realize that in that community, important decisions about what could and would be done were commonly made before and after the Sunday meeting. Not true for all of the United States, but true in many places, and certainly true in hers. But she didn't know this, thus there was no possibility of continuing off-the-record, informal, less-heated conversations with officials and other members of the community.

She also misunderstood the role of a do-it-yourself mentality that permeates many rural settings. Community leaders expected residents to do the best they could for themselves. If that doesn't work, then the community might pitch in and help. She had absolutely no understanding that the quickest, easiest, and safest course of action would have been to abate the dust herself. She could have oiled the road or installed additional sealed doors and windows, not to mention a more sophisticated air purification system, in her home.

What was of no help at all was that she continually reminded people how much money she had. Not only did such an attitude call into question her self-sufficiency ("Why spend general revenues for one person on one road when she could obviously do the job herself?"), it did not have its intended effect of one-upmanship or implied threat. Rural folks who have been in business for generations or who work a paid-for family farm or ranch might also have lots of bucks. Identifying such people is difficult for outsiders, but the lady persisted in her belief that she was financially superior.

The first 15 minutes of my initial conversation with the lady were spent listening to a tirade about how stupid, unreliable local service providers took advantage of her. A year after moving in, she *still* felt her problems were best dealt with via a phone call to "somebody." That the phone sometimes didn't work or that she was having trouble identifying that somebody really, really caused her distress.

In addition to dust, she was mightily bothered by traditional agricultural techniques that farmers employ. She saw them as foolish, unnecessary, and destructive to the environment. As far as I could determine, she grew up in urban Detroit with nary ever a visit to a real working farm or ranch. The realities of actual on-the-ground life in the country were lost on her. That farmers and ranchers were skilled small businesspeople with good, honest motives for their practices completely eluded this lady.

But there was more—much more. Garbage piled up simply because she didn't know how to bag it for transport. Then they were reluctant to haul it in their Lincoln to a distant county Dumpster because of the stench. There was no county conspiracy to keep her from dumping garbage, as she supposed.

Electrical power—especially during the winter months—frequently went down, justifiably terrifying the dear soul. She worried about heat and existing air purifiers not working. But there were no plans to ameliorate the situation by purchasing a standby generator and maintaining a supply of emergency fuel. Her only contingency was to get on the phone. Unfortunately, the phone also went down a lot.

Neighbor kids stole her plums, she said. It was raccoons, not neighbors—the nearest of which was over 3 miles away—but she wouldn't believe that. Even if she did, it wouldn't have mattered. She didn't like smelly skunks, pooping geese, rosebush-eating whitetail deer, and other critters. The fact that coyotes had eaten most of her house cats didn't help matters.

No plan was in place to keep all this abundant wildlife in its appropriate place. The couple owned some firearms, but these were intended to keep mythical rural rapists at bay. The last forcible rape in the county probably took place before they kept records of such things.

There were countless other examples. She failed to learn how to drive up and down rural roads (there is an established protocol), how to plan grocery purchases months in advance, and how to personally handle such problems as dead car batteries, clogged sewers, trees on the roof, snow removal, and catastrophic natural disasters such as fires and floods. We ended up parting ways when she announced that, in her experience, every human had some disgusting illegal perversion in their background. "Find out about the dead girl or live boy those commissioners and judges are sleeping with," she instructed. "That way I can march right in and force them to do their jobs."

"Too easy for small communities of busybody gossips to find out," I said. When I pointed out that older people who live all their lives in rural communities seldom have serious skeletons in their closets and that revealing such, even if they exist, will bring antagonism rather than cooperation, she fired me.

Again, this episode was the most complete in terms of serious problems converging in one place at one time. Certainly not all of this, or the items covered in the chapters to follow, apply to everyone in every rural situation. However, we are going to touch upon it all just in case the information might be helpful. On the one hand, neglecting any of these issues may not be terminal for adaptable, wise, and determined refugees from the city or suburbs. Yet taking it all into account will certainly add to the confidence and satisfaction of establishing a dream place in the country.

Some readers may not agree with my assessment of how things should be handled out in the country. This book is based on my experiences in particular communities in the American West and Midwest, but there very well may be regional and local customs, considerations, and twists in your patch of the woods. That's fine. The point is, by reading this book you will at least know that these issues exist and that some sort of handling is wise and necessary.

Now, let's get started.

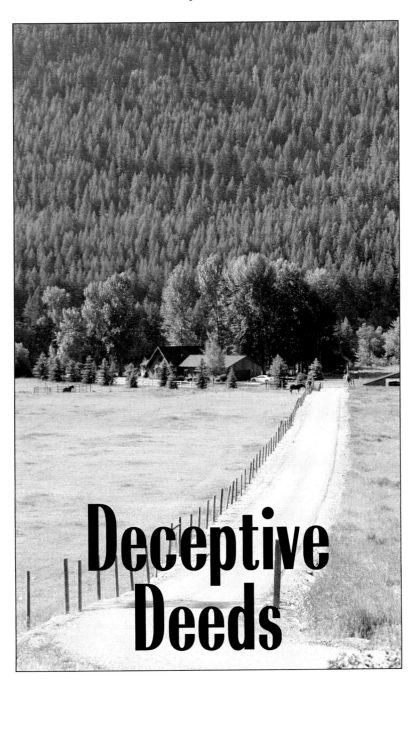

Chapter One

Deceptive
Deeds

Among remote rural burgs and communities, it is common to have one jack-of-all-trades worker to maintain roads, plow snow, clear storm drains, issue permits, oversee larger municipal contracts, catch errant dogs and cats, act as the local sheriff's representative, and even maintain community water and sewer systems if there are such.

Elmer Durham was one of those jack-of-all-trades public employees. Most often he made his presence and authority known by flashing a shiny tin badge discreetly pinned onto his bib overalls beneath a worn leather vest.

"Make U-turns on a side road, not on the main thoroughfare, sonny," were his first instructions to me, badge conveniently exposed.

Good to officially meet the gentleman, I thought. I also quit making any kind of U-turns even though the road in question carried perhaps 20 vehicles per day at most. Wise newcomers to any rural area take heed of admonitions from allegedly in-the-know locals, at least until time and further experience suggest otherwise.

Our second meeting was at 6:30 one Saturday morning. There was a sharp, official-sounding beating on our front door. Bedroom to front door, even from a dead sleep, took only an instant in our tiny cabin.

It was a mildly peeved Elmer Durham, ready to shake any residual sleep away with his surprising pronouncement.

"Your carport is built out into the middle of the road right-of-way," he informed. "You will have to get busy tearing it out. Can't have private structures in the middle of our roads."

Well, no, can't have that. But until his revelation, I had no clue.

It being Saturday and all, I unfortunately had to get the mayor out of bed and to the phone. Fortunately, coming from a small community background myself, I knew the vital importance of making his prior acquaintance. I politely and good-naturedly explained the situation to him and inquired whether I needed to break out the demolition tools after breakfast. He assured me that

I could have several additional days, weeks, or even months if necessary to figure out what was going on.

It's important to note how the exchange took place on the part of both parties. There was no hint of attorneys, citing of regulations, or red-faced confrontations. Such tactics work poorly in small, tightly knit rural areas. Hizzoner took the job only because no one else would, feeling it was his civic responsibility. No sense making his life miserable over something nobody really knew was a problem besides Elmer. The good mayor obviously felt the same toward me.

It took an additional couple of days, but subsequent investigation proved that, finesse and diplomacy notwithstanding, Mr. Durham was absolutely correct. The previous owners had, privately and perhaps recklessly, extended their massive concrete and brick carport out into the then unused and unopened county road.

But now I had bought myself some breathing room. By meeting with the mayor, Elmer, some county road people, the previous owners, title insurance people, and adjacent landowners, I was able to work everything out eventually. That was well over 30 years ago. The carport is still there in its original location.

So besides a brief tutorial in country manners, what is the important lesson here?

Rural deeds do not always accurately reflect what you see on the ground. Most legal descriptions and surveys of property these days are accurate, and searches by title insurance companies generally turn up any issues with liens, easements, water rights, and other sticking points. Yet three out of five pieces of rural property I have purchased have had defects similar to my carport episode. You must take this possibility into consideration when purchasing land in rural America.

This means bordering fences, rivers, ditches, power lines, and so forth might not be located within properly defined property lines. Roads, wells, springs, patches of timber, and rocky bluffs might not appear on the deed where they appear to be on the ground. These problems are exacerbated by the fact that there often is no one central place to go to check everything out for accuracy (although the county courthouse is the best place to start).

I once knew of some people who found that an ancient fence line put in scores of years back encroached onto their land by two rods (33 feet). The real property line now ran right through a poor old widow's garden and side porch. (Original settlers frequently did things like that, locating fences where most convenient rather than on exact property lines.) Now, the new owners were faced with the tremendously unpleasant task of exercising their legal property rights or being faced with not having enough land for an access right-of-way.

The new city folk in this case proved smarter than most. They elected not to incur community wrath, instead allowing the poor old soul to live out her life on their illegally appropriated property. They handled the situation with wisdom and finesse, thus avoiding a real can of worms. At the widow's death they straightened things out, but looking back, they sincerely wished they had avoided the whole mess by not getting into that land purchase in the first place.

These situations sometimes get dicey. Original roads may be so far off that adjoining owners may actually own a sliver of what you were led to believe was your own road frontage. Should differences arise, cranky neighbors could conceivably try to deny vital access to you. Even houses and barns can be built on the wrong spot, well outside the legally described property lines. There's often no way to tell by simply looking at the land.

The point is to anticipate these sorts of property rights snafus and know how to handle them. These issues can be worked out legally if one wishes to start life in a new community on such a sour note. Rather, differences of a few inches or feet can be worked out directly between well-meaning, nonconfrontational neighbors. If you, as the newcomer, fit this characterization, you should have no problems.

Beautiful, desirable property near lakes, streams, and rivers is most subject to property line problems. It occurs when the river, ditch, pond, or lake is used to define boundaries. But water is fluid. Adjoining land can change dramatically from year to year, even from season to season. I once owned a river-bottom farm in a flood plain that fluctuated in size as much as 5 acres per year! Fortunately, these "meander lines" are rarely, if ever, used to define property lines anymore. It's usually done by hard survey, but even these can be deceptive. Be dead certain important things such as structures, roads, wells, springs, streams, ponds, ditches, and whatever are really where they are supposed to be. Talk to the workmen about their survey work, even if it costs you money to do so. Visit the property with them. Have them locate a couple of corner pins and run some major property lines. (Keep in mind that some survey pins may not still be in their original, correct spots. Your surveyor should have some sense of this potential problem and will probably take his primary readings from geographical features, with the assistance of GPS and laser technology.) This is especially important when a divergence of a few feet could locate a valuable asset onto the land of a neighbor. I once narrowly avoided serious embarrassment when selling a patch of ancient elms killed by Dutch elm disease. Seems they were not mine to sell!

Another thing to do is, in a mild, nonconfrontational way, talk property lines with all adjacent landowners. You will gain nothing that is legally definitive or binding out of these conversations, but at least some hint of potential problem neighbors may surface. When property lines have been established a long time, most residents are comfortable with them. Adjoining landowners who've been there forever have been known to encroach on property that they have come to treat as their own. They don't want newcomers mucking things up making changes. Read between the lines, then investigate thoroughly.

County planners and assessors can be of some help so long as newcomers realize that rural residents tend to be suspicious of bureaucrats. Information from government workers may not be current or, for that matter, accurate. In a gentle, neighborly way, gather and sort through all information you are given.

Before purchasing anything, take the property description to both the courthouse and the title company. If yours is not a state that uses title insurance, you *and* an attorney should read the abstract. Make sure no easements, ancient or otherwise, are out there that significantly alter the property's utility to you. Huge, multiacre plots of land may not present much of a problem. Desirable features for which you are paying the big bucks may be buried sufficiently deep within the property lines that problems with them are unlikely. Give or take a little won't matter except if the property shares a border with a national forest, major road, or river. Again, you can't do enough research and checking.

Examples abound. A very wealthy land purchaser looking for ultimate seclusion found that somebody else held oil exploration rights dating to the 1930s on some property he wanted badly. They might not have been valid, but he backed out of the deal.

You might not think you will encounter a similar situation involving someone else's oil under your rec room, but you never know. Especially in the western United States, original owners sometimes sold all right, title, and interest to any oil, gas, minerals, and even gravel and clay lying beneath their property. Some of these contracts are still valid. Major ones will be recorded at the county assessor's office and certainly at the title insurance office. Frequently these claims lay dormant for decades. Nevertheless, they can be embarrassing and inconvenient. The lesson is that it's better to check now than to be surprised later!

Deceptive deeds and improper property lines aren't the only hazards. Planning and zoning regulations may preclude using your dream property as you wish. Local regs may prohibit building bridges and roads, drilling a well, or installing a septic. Don't find yourself ambushed by a bureaucratic decree after you've made plans—in your mind or in reality—for an important feature of your new abode.

Besides the details of your own parcel, you should also pay heed to what might be in store for surrounding property. You might have a million dollar view of the lake in the valley below your home but not realize that the land between your place and the water is zoned commercial and slated for future development. Again, you don't want a nasty surprise after you've established certain expectations for your new life in the country.

Zoning rules are items most city people are accustomed to dealing with. They are not, however, accustomed to dealing with things like discovering their well, road, or fence is on somebody else's land, which they cannot cross to perform routine maintenance. Knowing about these sorts of property issues beforehand and handling any problems early will save you a world of heartache down the road.

Chapter Two

Water

Transplanted city dwellers accustomed to turning on the tap for water—or calling a government worker when such is not forthcoming—are facing a new reality when they move to the country. The majority of rural properties in the United States do not suffer from serious water supply problems. Well size, location, and production generally take care of matters just fine. Still, pervasive water problems with which city people are unaccustomed to dealing are likely to pop up.

Of the last six homeowners to build up on the mountain within 2 miles of our place, two have had to drill wells costing roughly $20,000 each; three drilled two wells apiece. That's fine if you have the financial fortitude to absorb such costs; obviously not so good when straining to get the very last dollar into completing your dream home in the country. Well drillers are like attorneys: they will work faithfully till your last dollar is gone. Drilling multiple wells can very easily exceed any budget!

Another obviously important issue: you need to find out if you are even allowed to drill a well on your property. It varies by state, but some states require a certain amount of acreage before you can get a permit from the state engineer to drill a well. These permits might also restrict what you can use your well water for (e.g., you might be allowed to pump enough for normal home use but not for watering livestock or landscaping). An excellent resource for information on this and all other issues surrounding private wells can be found at www.wellowner.org.

Water systems for individual homeowners in the country are comprised of a well, a pipe extending down to a filter screen, and a water-lifting pump and pressure tank to hold water and pressurize the home's domestic piping. This is all in addition to the hot water heater, water softener, and water pipes inside the structure itself.

Typical household activity—taking showers, flushing toilets, washing clothes, and so forth—requires between 50 and 70 gallons of water per person per day. When grass and garden are also watered or a few head of livestock are involved, start thinking in standard well terms of a minimum of 3 to 5 gallons of water per minute. Five gallons per minute is the gold standard for most homeowners if the lawn, garden, and flowerbeds are relatively small.

Homeowners with well capacities on the low end of this requirement should consider installing a 1,000- to 2,500-gallon fiberglass holding tank. These systems mitigate for low-volume wells by continuously pumping water to the holding tank, thereby producing sufficient water over time.

Large water storage tanks have their pros and cons. They eat up valuable basement or yard space, cool or warm areas in which they are located, and may create dampness as well as produce stale-tasting water. On the plus side, holding tanks allow owners to purchase bulk water in town during times of drought or increased use cycles, like when the grandkids come to visit.

Determining if area wells are prone to go dry during some times of the year is relatively easy. Ask about commercial water supply services in the area. These are professionals who haul water to rural holding tanks at so much per thousand gallons. Where there is a need, these guys are present. A quick glance at the local yellow pages usually tells the tale. If they are listed, assume dry wells are common in the area.

This brings up another important issue city dwellers are usually unaccustomed to dealing with. Who you gonna call when the system goes down? Not the city or county—they have nothing to do with your well—and certainly not any apartment complex custodial hotline. Some jack-of-all-trade owners attempt their own repairs, but this is not always a valid plan in this era of rapidly changing and increasingly complex technology.

It's a basic article of faith that new rural homeowners must develop a close, even personal working relationship with their pump service people. I recommend talking to the seller in detail about who services the well, then call that person or firm. Talk at length with them about the specific system. Pay the biggest, best pump service company in the area to come out to look at the system. Listen to what they have to say. Try to get them to be candid and open. Two opinions on these matters are not too many!

States where water issues are difficult and convoluted may require that well logs be kept at a central office designated for that purpose. The county agent at the courthouse will know about these records, if they exist. Often older, smaller wells are not listed, but there is no harm in asking.

You also need to read between the lines when looking at the water system. Are there a number of company stickers that different repairmen leave after they make repairs? Are there none at all? Either case is a warning that the system needs too much work or hasn't had enough routine work done.

Some perfectly good, workable water systems draw out of lakes, rivers, and streams. No problem with these, other than the additional filters and purifiers that must be maintained. The limitations of these systems involve overt contamination—like a dead fish in the intake—and the need for frequent maintenance. Maintenance can be a real problem when water levels fluctuate, the climate is severe, or when something like passing boats or thawing ice physically damages the system.

What to do if you're looking at raw, wild, desolate land with no developed water supply? On the positive side, it is easier to make absolutely certain the well or water supply system is really on your own property because you will do it yourself. It doesn't happen often, but occasionally, due to faulty surveys, fraud, or good-old-boy accommodations, a well might not even be located on the property it serves. Those who drill their own wells can be certain it is actually on the property they own.

If the property you have in mind does not have a water system in place, you have a couple of options. First, ask the Realtor and current landowner/seller if they would be willing to develop water supplies on the lot you are considering, adding the actual costs to the sale price. The additional expense will be a bit higher than contracting the work yourself, but you will know for certain that domestic water is available before finalizing the deal. (You must ask them to prove they were successful before signing papers.) Owners and Realtors who are blowing smoke about ease of developing water will run for cover on hearing this one.

As an alternative to the above, which sellers seldom agree to, stipulate that the property will be purchased contingent on sufficient water being found and developed. Define the amount of water that is acceptable. This is not really as good as the first option, but it is probably the more realistic. You may sink $20,000 into a hole that's good only for an outhouse, but you will save the $250,000 expenditure for a home, not to mention $100,000 for the property itself.

Please keep in mind that, in many areas of the United States, mortgage loans on bare land that isn't fully paid for and is without proven water are almost impossible to get. In other words, without water and a paid-for lot, banks will not loan on the property.

Water is the subject of rural neighborhood gossip. Everybody uses it, everybody has problems with it, and everybody pretty much knows about any problems neighbors are having. As a new land purchaser, visit as many near neighbors as necessary to develop a picture of any issues you might face developing a new water supply on that specific piece of property. Then go right to the best local well driller and have a face-to-face talk with him. How many wells has he drilled in the area? What was the success ratio? What were the proven volumes? At what cost? Also talk about the size of well you require, its specific location, length of time to completion, amount of casing that will be required, and quality of water you can expect. Again, the Web site www.wellowner.org is a fine clearinghouse for all sorts of information on wells, including locating a reputable, licensed contractor for this work.

Water quality is an important issue, obviously. If your land is located near a farm, livestock yard, orchard, even a gas station, the potential is there for contamination from animal waste, pesticides, herbicides, and other impurities. Water samples can be sent to a commercial laboratory or taken to the local water company for testing. (Underwriters Laboratories, for example, has an excellent water-testing service called DrinkWell.) The water will be screened for impurities, dissolved solids, and other possible contaminants. Tales of health problems emanating from private rural wells are usually apocryphal and overblown, but it's still a good idea to check.

General information about water in the area is also available from the state hydrologist who, if such exists, may have his or her office at the state land grant college. Also try the largest full-service plumbing shop in the area, the county employee who approves new septic systems and issues permits for wells, and, of course, your friendly local pump man.

Be aware that some rural subdivisions, even extensive ones scattered over many acres, are watered by water user groups. Generally, these are private corporations formed to develop and deliver water to homeowner members. Homeowners band together to drill their own large central well, lay distribution pipe, and purchase pumps, switches, and electrical and pressurizing systems.

I am sure there is one out there somewhere, but I have never seen one of these that did not have extensive structural, mechanical, and legal problems. As a result, some states have developed strict rules and regulations regarding formulation, structure, reporting, and maintenance of these water user corporations. Best bet is to not assume anything when looking at a water co-op. Check on the system with at least six neighbors and two Realtors other than those offering the property. If you can get more opinions from pump service people, a well driller, and the county agent, even better. Search Internet or library news archives for items pertaining to any structural or legal hassles with the co-op or its water system.

Sounds like lots of work, but oh the grief I have seen! Your entire home and property may only be worth the amount left after subtracting costs of rectifying a severely damaged water users' association.

Water issues are not all related to having or not having water in sufficient abundance. There may be more than enough water and still be surprises and problems to overcome.

Ursula Kipling bought a beautiful, well-tended country estate some 30 miles west of Boise, Idaho. Along with her scenic property she acquired an obligation to pay an irrigation association assessment of $16 per month in perpetuity. This was the result of an old, legally binding irrigation contract on the original piece of ground. Adding insult to injury, water for which she paid was no longer available to her, had she even wanted it. Apparently, numerous subdivisions of the original property removed the actual waterway from her plot without removing her obligation to pay. Ursula was an attorney, and even she found that, as a practical matter, she could not have the assessment waived or lifted. Mucking around with the mess was more trouble than it was worth, she finally concluded.

If the original concrete ditch that created the problem had still run across her property, could Ms. Kipling have taken some water to freshen her front lawn? Maybe, maybe not. Water, and the rights thereto, are hotly protected in many parts of the United States. She could have incurred serious problems by even allowing her kids to swim in the ditch, much less actually take water from it.

Ursula sincerely wished she had known about this water situation before purchase, yet nothing showed up on the title report or the deed or as a result of talking with the Realtor and seller. The first she knew anything was amiss was when bills started popping up demanding payment. Although knowing about the issue would have been helpful, most likely she would have purchased anyway, she admits.

Here's another problem: too *much* water. Tom and Terry Tate of Lagro, Indiana, bored a simple 1.5-inch well pipe down 30 feet, tapping into all the domestic groundwater they could possibly use. It put out some 5 gallons per minute . . . but it wasn't that easy. Spring runoff floodwaters overtopped their well, seriously contaminating it and damaging their pump. They had located a good, inexpensive supply of water, but the new well was still in the wrong place because of this unforeseen complication.

Existing water equipment can be a problem. A young couple moved into a delightfully rugged stone house in rural New Jersey. Built in the early 1800s, it had been heavily remodeled and wisely modernized several times. Everything was new—except the water pump, controls, pressure tank, and delivery pipes. Rust and calcium from their shallow well so corroded and constricted their home's already inadequate half-inch galvanized delivery pipe that they had to tear up yard, flowerbeds, rock gardens, and even the foundation wall to install new piping. Over and above the expense, it was especially unsettling to have to do this ugly work only four weeks after moving in.

Although money solves lots of problems in the country, this one came on the heels of several other unanticipated events. Taken together, they nearly bankrupted the couple. At best it was a huge disappointment.

Water for rural neophytes is a complex, far-ranging subject with which they are unused to dealing. Speak with as many knowledgeable people as possible about your specific property. Hire people to help if necessary. When it comes to rural water, there is value in many opinions.

Chapter Three

Septic Systems

*L*ike most new transplants to the country, Jim Pittford gave little thought to his plumbing. He flushed or pulled the plug and the problem disappeared.

Everything came undone one crackling winter day. Simultaneously, his sinks, wash kitchen drains, and toilets plugged up tight. Mr. Pittford had no clue what caused the sudden problem. There were no prior warnings till an ugly, stinking mess erupted onto his bathroom floor. Ruined a rug in one section and lifted the linoleum in another, he recalls.

Not only did Mr. Pittford have no clue about the cause, curing what was obviously a horrible problem was completely beyond him. "I had no place to go!" he later claimed, a terrible pun given only half in jest.

No unanticipated problem that rural dwellers might have to deal with is more disgusting, difficult, and distracting than a sudden stoppage of a home's waste disposal—i.e., septic—system. That's the first lesson for city slickers accustomed to letting municipal authorities handle these kinds of problems. (It is, however, untrue that septic tanks have minds of their own, sensing when it is a long weekend over a holiday with a full complement of houseguests and choosing that specific time to act up.)

Solving this problem is generally not a do-it-yourself affair. The vast majority of people will have to call in professional help. Septic tank maintenance and repair people are accustomed to anguished calls from rural residents at all times of the day and night. Having to pay for emergency repairs can get expensive . . . until one has a better understanding of a typical septic system. In other words, if you do some homework beforehand, it is infinitely easier and cheaper to talk to septic system companies regarding remedies and prevention.

Basic septic tank construction, function, and maintenance are not particularly difficult. Perhaps because these systems lie buried out of sight underground, they are a mystery for most folks, including many rural ones. But you've got to know the basics to get along with your country plumbing!

Start with the obvious fact that wastewater of all sorts is collected in the home's waste system and drained out somewhere. In the suburbs and city, that "somewhere" is the handy, taxpayer-funded sewer system. In the sticks, it's a large, tub-like structure called a septic tank, which is connected to a drain field (also known as a leach or absorption field). Septic tanks are holding containers of 1,000 or more gallons buried about a foot beneath the ground anywhere from 10 to 40 or so feet from the house, space and topography permitting. Our tank is located 40 feet from the house at the edge of the gravel parking area, conveniently covered with 12 inches of loose gravel for easy access. (Serious problems could occur, though, if we ever sold our place without telling the new owners about the septic's location. What if they unknowingly paved or blacktopped over the tank? More on this later.)

Many older septic tanks were made of tar-coated, heavy-gauge steel. Today they are all concrete or fiberglass. If you are installing a new system, don't ever use anything but concrete for the septic tank. It will last 50 or 60 years. Fiberglass tanks are complete junk, in my opinion.

Tank size is a matter of expected use. If it's a two or three bedroom home, 1,000 gallons is okay. Septic tanks for large-occupancy homes with toilets attached to every bedroom should be installed with greater capacity, perhaps 2,500 gallons. Some experts claim an overly large, underused septic tank may dry up and die, killing beneficial bacteria that does the job of breaking down waste products. I haven't seen this happen, but do consult with local experts if you are installing a new system. At any rate, never, ever underbuild.

Wastewater drains from the house's plumbing system into the septic, where it hits a baffle within the tank that slows its velocity. Once wastewater enters the tank, it is mightily worked on by bacteria within. Solids sink to the bottom as "sludge" or float to the surface, forming a heavy scum layer. As is the purpose of the tank, most of these solids are liquefied and subsequently moved around an outlet baffle in the back of the tank until it travels downstream to the drain field, where it passes through a small diversion box that channels the effluent into the perforated pipes that encompass the leach system. Not all older systems have a diversion box, but most modern systems do.

Nonorganic material—including bits and pieces of plastic, broken glass, jewelry, stones, and similar material inadvertently flushed down the drain—settles in the tank's heavy sludge layer. The tank must be pumped periodically to clear out all this junk, plus accumulated organic waste that has not decomposed. We pump our septic tank once every 10 to 12 years, even though most experts recommend doing it every 3 to 5 under normal conditions. Cost at this writing is between $75 and $300, depending on your location.

Depending on the soil type and topography of your land, a drain field can be anything from a couple of lines of special perforated plastic pipe laid out in a trench, which is subsequently buried, to a deep, gravel-lined trench with pipe running along inside. Three vital aspects of septic drain fields should be kept in mind.

First, never deploy less than one foot of drain field pipe per gallon of septic capacity—e.g., a 1,000-gallon septic must install with no less than 1,000 feet of drain field pipe. Often in poorly drained soils or under other less-than-perfect conditions, it is much more. Drain fields are very inexpensive, so don't cut corners. Good ones last years!

Second, know that purifying bacterial action continues in the drain field. Bury it too shallow and it can freeze in colder climates or create a stinking, unsanitary wet spot in your yard. Bury it too deep and vital oxygen will be hopelessly choked away from the field, reducing its ability to perform properly.

Third, drain fields absolutely must be kept away from domestic water wells. No compromise on this issue. No one wants septic effluent in his or her drinking water. Same goes for natural water sources that feed into the regional water supply. The water company inspects all properties located on reservoir watershed land and will confront homeowners with ongoing leach field troubles.

How far away? Distance recommendations vary depending on soil and subsoil composition, volume of discharge, depth of the well, topography, county requirements, and many other factors. I suggest a minimum of 150 feet from the well and at least 100 feet from the high water mark of any water source (stream, pond, etc.) on the property.

If you will be installing a new septic system, be absolutely sure that the lot you are purchasing has enough space to accommodate a septic tank and drain field that will not encroach upon your well and other water sources. Get opinions from a septic tank installer, plumber, neighbor, and/or county sanitation personnel about this, not the land seller or real estate agent.

While you are evaluating the land in terms of a septic system, it is wise to analyze the nature of the soil as well. In many cases—especially those involving the construction of large, expensive, multifamily homes—one can hire a backhoe operator to dig a minimum of an 8-foot-deep hole someplace on the lot. Look carefully to see what is down there. Is it solid rock? Are there moist sublayers, indicating there may be springs in the area? What you discover will pertain to drainage, aeration, and other elements of your septic system and therefore how and where you construct it.

Where soil types vary widely, it may be wise to run a percolation test on your piece of heaven. Commonly called "perc tests," many county health officials require them. Perc tests are simply post holes drilled in the ground to a prescribed depth, into which a measured amount of water is poured. How long it takes this water to soak away provides the test results, i.e., whether drainage is too fast, too slow, or within accepted parameters for the area. These tests are not standardized, and some county perc standards, particularly in rural California, are held to unrealistic levels in an attempt to stop all rural development. Your septic installer will know about these.

Septic professionals claim that lost septic systems are a familiar problem. Many homeowners fresh out of the sewer-connected city or suburbs have absolutely no clue where their septic tank and drain field are located. Some can't even affirm with certainty that they actually have a septic system buried on their property, this in spite of the fact that snow will melt on top of modern, shallow tanks and drain fields in winter, and grass is greener and taller there in summer.

Homeowners who can locate their own tanks and uncover the access holes (there are three inspection/cleanout holes in the top of the tank, one each over the inlet and outlet baffles and one in the center to facilitate pumping) will save themselves time and money when it comes time to pump it out. Have the exact location of your septic system written down and stored in a convenient place so it (the septic) can always be located in an emergency. If you are installing a new system, draw up a precise, easy-to-read map, make numerous copies, and keep them in logical locations so any household member can get their hands on one in an emergency.

There's one more small item. City people are plagued by credit card solicitations; country people suffer at the hands of salespeople touting septic tank additives. But does this stuff really work?

In my opinion, not to the extent that you would want to lay out large sums of money for it. We have always flushed a box of inexpensive Rid-Ex down the stool immediately after pumping the septic. That's all we do. As mentioned, we go about 12 years on a pump job. Rid-Ex is available off your grocer's shelf in most rural areas. Otherwise, perhaps the best way to maintain a healthy septic system is ensure that only waste and soapy water enter it (you can even go as far as disconnecting the garbage disposal and starting a compost pile instead) and never pour grease into it.

All this might sound complicated, expensive, and disgusting, but it seldom is for informed rural residents. Given a modern, properly installed cement septic tank and a drain field of adequate size for your situation, problems with waste disposal are probably less than city dwellers experience with their sewers. All you have to do is keep track of your septic's location and maintenance schedule, plus the number of a local pumping service. Pretty soon, you will be like most rural folks and come to look at septic tank service as a fairly routine procedure.

Chapter Four

The Road
to Paradise

You have found the perfect piece of property on which to build a dream home in the country. Water, topography, and climate are perfect. Places for the lawn, dahlia beds, vegetable garden, and pond are easy to visualize. Gentle breezes blow through giant trees. It is so peaceful you are fearful lest the quiet keep you awake at night.

"People pay big money for a drop-dead view like this," your Realtor effuses. Not a terribly instructive statement, since you have already seen the asking price. Still, marriage to this particular piece of real estate looks imminent.

But keep one truth in mind: to a tremendous extent, you will be marrying the road to your property rather than the property itself.

In other words, rural property is rural. You gotta go to town for stuff. Whether we are talking about the construction or moving phase (if it's an existing home), you will virtually be burning up the road between your place and town. The condition of that road will become a major factor in the quality of your new life in the country.

There are three basic types of country roads: gravel, dirt, and hard surface. These roads are either public—meaning responsibility for upkeep technically rests with the county—or private, meaning upkeep is your job.

Government maintenance of rural roads—grading, snow plowing, gravel replacement, pothole filling, and all that—is a mixed bag. First, there are public roads that the authorities may or may not maintain. They should maintain them, but this is not a perfect world. In many jurisdictions, regular county roads are not maintained at all—no plowing, no grading, no gravel replacement, no nothing. Second, there are private lanes (think of these as long, extended driveways) that the county definitely will not maintain. Unless something extraordinary can be worked out, each homeowner will be responsible for his or her own lane.

Public road maintenance is performed on a priority basis, and the county workers' priorities are not always the same as your priorities.

Keep in mind that these priorities can change surprisingly quickly in response to local conditions that have nothing to do with the weather. One time, a close friend won a county commissioner's election in a surprise upset. Next morning after the election, he was jarred awake by noisy county graders working on his road. No grading or maintenance had been done on that road for years. Obviously, county priorities had changed the previous night.

Assuming you are not such an influential member of the community, you must rely on more proactive measures. First, know that you may have to purchase a four-wheel-drive vehicle, a set of tire chains, tractor and plow, or ATV to negotiate county roads in poor condition. Frequently it's all of the above, especially if your private access lane or the road from town to your house is long and exposed.

The next thing to do is to ask about maintenance and snow removal at the county highway district office. Don't be surprised if things haven't changed in the past 60 years and that there is still no enticement to bring the plow up your way. You, as a newcomer on a poorly built or unmaintained rural road, may not be greeted with the joy and enthusiasm you might expect. Your requests to upgrade the road or put it on the regular county maintenance schedule may very well be refused or ignored.

So what to do if your road is closed by a spring flood, winter ice storm, summer windstorm, or whatever? First, don't call the highway department to gripe or explain your busy, important schedule. Newcomers who violate this rule will find that their specific road's priority has slipped to dead last. Rather, here is how to proceed wisely and effectively.

Call your highway people to ask how things are going and how they are weathering the crisis. "Is there anything I can do to help?" you ask. There probably won't be, but the offer will portray you as someone willing to pitch in rather than someone demanding service. Usually the nice person on the other end will volunteer when he thinks the roads will be cleaned and opened, without your putting him on the spot by asking directly.

When they do come to make repairs or clean debris, greet road workers with a smile, a pot of coffee, and, if possible, fresh donuts or baked bread. At Christmas, consider taking a nice card and box of expensive chocolates down to the county highway department office. Make sure they realize who you are and where you live. These gestures should be subtle but genuine—certainly don't demand a quid pro quo, and don't be gushing or phony about the whole affair either. You're just another neighbor and member of the community who appreciates their hard work. Do this correctly and you may not move to the top of the list, but you won't be on the bottom either.

Here's an old trick that might be worth trying. I grew up at the end of a 200-yard private lane on a Midwestern farm. When raging snowstorms blanketed us and we couldn't turn a wheel through four-foot drifts, granddad sometimes placed a pint of nice Scotch on the fence post at the end of the lane by the barn lot. County plow operators frequently took the bait. They plowed in to retrieve the bottle and then out again. Who knows, it might still work today if the plow operator happens to know there's a jug for the taking at the end of your driveway! (This gambit is best attempted if you know the person with whom you're dealing. If the plow man is a nondrinking Mormon, for instance, you're likely to offend rather than impress him with your idea of off-the-book relations.)

Some road cleaning jobs can be handled privately by you and your neighbors without having to rely on the county's schedule. Cutting up fallen trees or plowing persistent snow drift areas are examples. It doesn't take much to learn how to operate a chain saw or a pickup with mounted plow blade, and such private handling of duties that the government takes care of in other places is one of the hallmarks of self-sufficient country life. Certain tasks are such that the authorities don't want private residents fooling with them, and rightly so in most cases. Repairing a damaged bridge over a creek or removing electrical wires are good examples.

No matter who handles the maintenance, they will be dealing with various conditions that are ubiquitous to virtually all rural roads. Snow-packed, icy conditions in the winter are a given everywhere except in the warmer South, but spring break-up in some places in rural America is worse than winter snows. Certain soil types require infinitely more ballast (i.e., underlying fill material) than others. If they are not properly ballasted, deep holes capable of swallowing whole SUVs can emerge with the spring thaw. Fixing these dangerous, gaping holes is extremely expensive, not to mention building roads in places that create these conditions in the first place.

Repeated rolling of wheels over nonpaved country roads creates a syndrome called washboarding, where closely spaced, corrugated ripples traverse the road. Washboarding creates a bumpy, shaky ride that can quickly become hazardous if you drive too fast. As your tires bump off the washboard surface at speed, they lose traction with the road, causing your vehicle's back end to fishtail if you're not careful. Drive slowly over washboard conditions, especially around curves, and you will have no problems.

Washboarding can be eliminated by grading, but no matter how well maintained an upaved road, there will always be some section that becomes washboardy or potholed or both.

During dry times, dirt and gravel roads can be extremely dusty. This can become a significant problem if you are building or buying a home near such a road. To mitigate the effects of dust, you can install central air conditioning with electrostatic filters or other special air filtering equipment. Another option is to call in a professional road oiler and have him coat your little section of dusty road with oil. Road oilers are listed in the Yellow Pages or can be found on the Internet. You can also try the county road people for leads. Cost at this writing can be as little as 11 cents per square foot. You can also do it yourself with commercially available dust-control products, which run about $5 a gallon

But be vigilant. Shyster road-oilers are still out there. I have been sold a phony water-soluble material that did little good for 30 days and nothing after that. Another oiler ran only a narrow 8-foot band down the center of the road. "Oh, you want the whole road oiled? Costs twice as much to oil the whole thing," he said.

Maybe you don't wish to put up with any of this and yearn for a good old reliable paved road like you had back in the suburbs. Before you lobby to have the gravel road in front of your home upgraded to pavement, note that hard-surfaced rural roads are not necessarily better! Long-time rural residents know this. Here is why. Every county highway department throughout the United States has severe budget problems. For this reason, paved county roads are frequently hard surfaced to minimum standards. Deterioration starts quickly and may reach drastic levels before subsequent repairs are made. In other words, blacktop in front of your property may get so bad, a plain gravel or even dirt road may be easier to drive on and maintain in the long run. Also, when there is ice and snow, loose gravel tends to break up slick spots, creating safer travel conditions.

While you are figuring out the intricacies of public road maintenance in your area, you might as well turn your attention to your private lane as well. A good, solid private road to your property is essential. If you are building your dream home in the woods from scratch, construction supply trucks need to make it in safely and reliably. Later, you have to think about fire and emergency vehicles as well as routine deliveries of such things as fuel oil and LP gas. United Parcel Service and FedEx delivery people also need to feel welcome.

In most cases, a road will already run out to your new property. If not, keep soils in mind when evaluating lane building projects lying ahead. Wet, swampy areas, for instance, will require numerous corrugated drainpipes to carry water from one side to the other. Figure at least $45 each for 8-inch, homeowner-sized culverts 20 feet long. Larger culverts that pass under a road can cost thousands or even tens of thousands of dollars to put in.

Exercise great caution when installing culverts or bridges to bypass bodies of water, or even when filling small potholes or low, water-soaked areas. Fooling around with wetlands—even property that may be *construed* as wetlands—carries great risk if nosy environmental groups or state wetland bureaucrats get wind of it. Such work requires licenses, approvals, and permits, and the rules and regulations seem to change weekly.

Some country residents believe small culverts or a bit of fill hidden back away from obvious bodies of water will be overlooked, but don't count on it. It is up to individual landowners to make their own decisions regarding these matters and proceed at their own risk. Better to ask at the appropriate county offices or talk to neighbors before assuming or doing anything. When it comes to doing roadwork around wet areas, I have found that informal conversations with county workers such as road grader or dump truck operators are helpful. Not the final word, but helpful.

Like public roads, private lanes require maintenance in the form of removing snow, grading away washboards, filling potholes, and similar tasks. Snow removal is accomplished with a plow mounted to a suitable vehicle (pickup truck, ATV, etc.) or a snow blower operated by hand for shorter driveways, by vehicle for longer ones (we attach our snow blower to the tractor). Routine grading can be accomplished by doing it yourself with a tractor and grader, hiring a neighbor with a tractor and grader, or using improvised equipment if you have the hand for it. For years we maintained our lane by pulling a 10-foot piece of heavy railroad iron up and down to smooth it. We used our Jeep or truck as a pull vehicle.

If your private lane is dirt, note that precipitation of any sort will often make it impassable. Drive on it anyway and it will rut so badly that it will become virtually impassable after drying out. Turning a dirt road into a more reliable all-weather route requires an application of gravel. Road gravel is either crushed from solid rock or dug out of a gravel pit. Specifications are made on the basis of gravel size. Steep, mountainous roads require smaller sized gravel; larger gravel tends to roll downhill, collecting in giant sand traps of sorts.

Because road gravel is ubiquitous to rural life, you will probably have no trouble finding several sellers and haulers. Look in the phone book for listings or inquire at local lumberyards. But be forewarned. Sometimes gravel must be hauled from great distances in great lumbering trucks at great expense. Price for the stone is usually figured by volume, with delivery and spreading fees built in.

No matter how bad your rural roads might get, take solace in knowing that even those in the absolute worst condition are not even in the same league as those that pass for public transportation byways in places like India or even nearby Mexico. Explore your options with the local authorities, know what you and your neighbors are capable of handling yourselves, and be prepared to handle any sort of road condition and you'll do just fine.

Chapter Five

Electrical Power

The purchase of a portable standby generator for Erik Grupp of Kodiak, Alaska, might seem strange at first. Grupp lived well within the confines of the city of Kodiak itself, not out in a wild, remote area.

Still, Kodiak is notorious for its sudden, intense storms, so Grupp figured life there was inordinately risky without his own generator. "It's a miracle," Grupp reports, "that power interruptions occur as infrequently as they do." Perhaps because the power company expected such and were appropriately staffed and equipped, outages tended to be brief—from four hours to a day in length, max. The problem was the frequency with which residents had to endure them.

Without reliable power, Grupp's extensive frozen food supplies were jeopardized in summer. During the bitter cold winter months, he felt he risked the comfort and safety of his family in a power outage of any duration. Homes in his area, subjected to howling winds straight out of the North Pole, have frozen up in 90 minutes without the relatively small amounts of electricity necessary to power the oil furnace and blower. Acquiring a standby generator seemed the prudent thing to do.

Generators are one of those appliances that require a reason, or perhaps even an excuse, for ownership. They are sufficiently expensive that most folks, including rural ones, don't just go out and buy one. The common reasoning for having one is recognition that rural power is fairly reliable in most areas, but when it does go down, consequences can be severe. There is also the matter of using a generator to run labor-saving power tools in the travel camper or shop, or out on the grounds away from an electrical outlet.

Peter Williams lives in a very rural, almost primitive place called Harvard, Idaho. Williams also purchased a standby generator recently. Fire danger in the deep, dry forests within which Williams lives is his most immediate concern. "I really need a generator to operate my well and pond pump in case we have a forest fire and all power is cut off," he says. It is not an uncommon concern in his neck of the woods.

Waiting to purchase a generator till the hour of desperate need is not a smart plan. Doing so usually leads to an ill-considered, inappropriate unit not well suited for your specific needs. There is also no question that the generator will cost materially more money in times of emergency, when intense demand drives prices up.

When purchasing a standby generator, realize that one size definitely does not—and never will—fit all. If nothing else, we know this from the many makes, models, and sizes of generators available. The Northern Tool and Equipment catalog, for instance, has eight pages listing more than 50 different generators. Given the fact that research and analysis are necessary parts of a generator purchase and that rural safety and convenience should be priorities in your new life, starting the process early is wise.

My first generator back on the farm was a tractor power take-off model rated at 4,000 watts. Figure about 2 horsepower will generate 1,000 watts of reliable, continuous output on this or any other type of generator. My tractor was rated at 45 horsepower, suggesting I could have driven a much larger generator had I wished. But our power needs were relatively modest at that time, almost as modest as our financial ability to purchase a generator. Without freezers and deep well pumps, our electrical needs were few; all we really did with the rig was run the welder. At one point before the generator, we lived, without complaint, for four days without any electrical power.

Rural neophytes who plan to purchase a standby generator have several decisions to make. The first is to determine how large a generator is required to keep your urgently required appliances in operation. Keep in mind the fact that, for most of us, life will not go on as usual when the standby generator is supplying the power. The reality is that, other than a few essential appliances, every other plug will be pulled.

Commonly, rural residents will need to pump water, preserve food (as in freezers and refrigerators, which can and normally do run intermittently), power the furnace and blowers in winter, and run a few lights. (Minimal lighting, we have found, is more neces-sary than most people suppose. The many hours of work needed to hold the ranch together make it a necessity, particularly in northern winters when days are short and conditions severe.) Using generators to power up an electric oven (about 5,000 watts), washing machine (500 watts), space heater (1,500 watts), toaster (1,000 watts), or even hot water heater (4,000 watts) is an extravagance few will likely consider. Forget luxuries like the elec-tric can opener, yard lights, and ice machine.

Deep well pumps require about 1,200 watts, gas or oil fur-naces and blowers about 1,000 watts, chest freezers 1,000 watts when running, and lights marginally more than what is written on the bulb. That not all these appliances need to run at once sug-gests that many homeowners could get by with 6,000 watts of generating capacity in emergency circumstances! In the case of freezers, for instance, running time need be only six to eight hours per day. Run other stuff when the freezers are silent. If the ambi-ent temperature outside is, well, freezing, and the freezer is locat-ed in an unheated garage, you might not have to hook it up to the generator at all.

In actual practice, it always takes a bit more power than first supposed, and it is unnecessarily tough on a generator to run it at full capacity for extended periods. In that regard, purchase only a continuous duty model, preferably one of the industrial units.

Most manufacturers recommend 8 to 9 kilowatts to run an average household in an emergency, a figure I have found from experience to be just right. Purchasing additional capacity in a generator does no harm, but 8 to 9 kilowatts is a good figure.

Next, determine if the generator will be deployed as a central unit to power the entire household from one location, or is it best in your circumstances to move it around, essentially powering one appliance at a time. In many situations it makes sense to use two or three smaller, portable generators on what amounts to an indi-vidual basis to power the well pump, freezer, lights, or whatever. This plan avoids the high cost of a larger generator, allowing pur-chase of one smaller generator now and others in the future as need suggests and finances allow. (Smaller generators are also convenient to have around for use in the travel camper, on construction sites, in the shop, or when just out tent camping.) On the downside, moving all these generators around and servicing them can be time consuming and tedious. At the hour of need, time is always at a premium.

Large central generators can have the advantage of being less obvious, both audibly and visibly, if set up in a location dedicated to their housing and operation. Once installed, they are convenient to start, run, and service. In most cases wheel kits can be installed, adding a bit of mobility, but is a 460-pound, 15-kilowatt, 25-horsepower, central generator ever really portable?

There is also an important safety issue when using large generators as a standby source of power. If you connect your generator to your home's power grid, you *must* isolate it from the grid *before* going live. If not, when you heat up your home wiring you will also be heating up the electrical grid on your side of the breach—and risk blowing some poor lineman off the pole, who is unaware that your side of the break is hot. If there's any possibility your generator will feed power back into the grid, shut off the main circuit breaker to your house or pull your main box fuses and hide them away so they cannot be reinstalled intentionally or by accident. As with any large electrical appliance, make sure you understand your generator's safe and proper operation before you need it in an emergency.

At one time China Diesel offered small, 8-horsepower, 4-kilowatt generators. Nice units these, but only I could turn the starting crank with enough enthusiasm to fire the engine. Which leads to the next decision: does one purchase an electric start unit or rely on muscle power? It depends entirely on who might be called on to put the generator in service in an emergency. My rule of thumb is that any engine over 10 horse should be electric start. Generators sit around most of the time. Starting a cold engine after it had just spent 14 months in a storage shed is always difficult. Because my wife and daughter might be called upon to fire up our generator, ours are all electric start. We just need to remember to replace the batteries every four years—an added maintenance expense, but worth it.

Picking the correct fuel for the generator is another consideration. I store 1,000 gallons of diesel fuel with which to heat our home and fuel my tractors and truck. Diesel-powered generators are significantly more expensive, but they are longer lived in continuous service. Gallon for gallon, more power is generated on less fuel. In my case, choosing diesel fuel for my generator was a no-brainer.

A medical doctor living in the valley on the other side of our mountain elected to purchase a liquid propane (LP) gas-powered generator. He also purchased and installed a 1,000-gallon LP tank. (Leased LP gas tanks are risky in an emergency situation, he says, because it puts you at the mercy of the supplier.) In a truly tough situation, his unit can also operate on plain gasoline. There is charm in such diversity!

Knowing when to deploy the standby generator is more art than science. No one likes to go through all the work getting everything set up, only to have the power come back on. Talk to your new neighbors to determine how widespread an outage really is. Local radio may have some information, and it may be possible to call the power company for their estimate of when power will be restored (but be prepared for vague or evasive answers—and sometimes they just don't know). Unless there is a fire danger or some other mitigating circumstance, our rule of thumb is to wait four hours before deploying the generator.

Not too many years ago, our power went down after an accident on the highway took out a substation. Apparently there were other problems with power lines out in the county that exacerbated the situation. After three days on the generator, our power company informed us it would be at least three more days before we were restored.

The continued noise and smell of the generator finally got to my daughter, so she devised a plan. She called the power company, and in her sweetest, most polite tone, said, "My dad thinks he knows what the problem is. Is it okay if he climbs up the pole and fixes our power himself?"

A power company truck and crew pulled up our drive within 20 minutes of the call.

Chapter Six

Communications

A late winter snowstorm swirled outside the windows, dumping at least 8 inches around our home. This storm was a bit different, though. It isn't unheard of to experience thunder and lightning during a snowstorm, but it is unusual, at least in these parts.

Suddenly, while we stood dumbly looking out the windows, a particularly healthy bolt of lightning hit our phone line someplace up the mountain. There was snapping and crackling inside our office, alerting us to the fact that maybe we had a real problem.

Usually we disconnect our phone lines and the electricity into the office computer in anticipation of arriving electrical storms. At one time we didn't even use surge protectors, nor were we diligent about unplugging. During this particular lightning storm we had two excellent Belkin surge protectors hooked in series, guarding the phone and computer lines. The strike was so close and powerful it blew out *both* surge protectors, but our computer, fax, answering machine, and printers were spared from damage.

Later we tried calling the phone company to see if the fault rested with their equipment. Let me tell you, dealing with them was worse than having our e-mail cut off or going through the trouble of getting our spare surge protection out of storage and us back online. A phone company employee in Phoenix (at least 1,500 miles away) kept insisting it was impossible that an electrical strike had actually come in through our phone line to take out the surge protectors. I was tempted, but I didn't send the damaged surge protectors to her so she could see for herself. (Belkin, on the other hand, graciously replaced our damaged units at no cost other than postage.)

Even for experienced rural residents like ourselves, being suddenly cut off from the outside world is traumatic (almost as traumatic as dealing with phone company people in Phoenix). One immediately thinks about how to summon help should grandma or one of the grandkids have a problem when the phone is still on the fritz, but of course these simultaneous emergencies seldom, if ever, actually arise.

Established rural residents expect to lose their phone service every now and then. Everybody out in the country with long, exposed phone lines is in the same boat. Some make extensive preparations to overcome this difficulty. A few just go with the flow, accepting a few days of isolation from what they consider to be acts of God.

Loss of phone service places the need for a reliable, all-weather vehicle in sharp focus, especially in households with folks in less than 100 percent good health. Assumptions that you could make it to town during an especially violent storm in the family two-wheel drive sedan may go right in the tub. It's okay to have a borderline rural vehicle when the grass is green and the birds are singing, but definitely not when a howling tornado or violent rainstorm comes blasting through.

Cell phones can be a partial answer. At a minimum, those with their landlines down can report their loss of service. This assumes cell phone service is available *and* works reliably in your area—not always realistic assumptions in rural America.

Although cell service is rapidly expanding to many rural areas, it will never be as reliable in the country as in cities for some time yet. Rural topography guarantees it, not to mention sparse populations of people providing a smaller market and therefore less incentive for service providers to expand deep into the mountains and countryside. Plan on maintaining a landline until reliable cell phone service is available in every corner of the United States (which it might be by the time you read this book).

Some city transplants do not take the time to be sure their cells work out in the boonies at their new digs. That's a mistake. Don't wait until the hour of dire need and assume cell phone service will be available to you at the press of a button. Take your cell out to the property to try it. Maybe it works only at the corner of the lot, or up the road a few hundred yards, or at the top of the hill out back. Even this is something when there is an emergency and nothing else is working, but it's hardly a convenient arrangement.

Some people feel they must go to great lengths to stay connected to the outside world. We have a neighbor who is a two-way ham radio guru. There is no question that he could make emergency calls on his radios, but is reaching somebody in Chile or the Yukon Territory much help? There just aren't that many ham radio operators out there relative to the general population, so the chances of your reaching someone in your area during an emergency are slim. Given the troubles and expense of establishing a ham radio system and its questionable general utility, I wonder if this is a practical approach.

As a partial vindication of my position, this fellow has since gone to cell phones in a big way. Both he and his wife carry them. Each has their separate line, and they both carry tiny backup phones in the event their main phones crash. Probably overkill, but they do like to stay in touch.

We tried two-way "2-meter" radios for a while. These were better than hand-held CBs, which were complete nonstarters—too much extraneous traffic, limited range, and the radios themselves lacked durability. In the case of 2-meter radios, keeping up with regulatory requirements was a hassle. Range and reliability were only marginally better than CBs. We also faced the same dilemma our friend the ham operator faced. In an emergency, who would we call with our 2-meter units who could actually help? I certainly couldn't use them to call the phone company to report our service was out.

Some rural folks actually enjoy the mystique and seclusion that comes with being totally cut off from the outside world. Not everyone is similarly disposed. In times past, country people have tried all sorts of methods to deal with a break in communications. Early inhabitants of the mountainous West sometimes signaled U.S. Forest Service planes when they needed help by hoisting a prearranged flag or banner on their flagpole. When I was young, my aged grandparents had a system where they placed a floodlight in the living room window to alert neighbors to the fact that they needed help. That was fine so long as the power was not out at the same time as the phone.

Electronics mavens like to talk about phone and Internet service organized through their television satellite dishes. My understanding is that such is currently available for those willing to pay high monthly fees. Perhaps this service will come down in price, and perhaps the power won't go out the same time as the phone, or you will have a standby generator. So far, receiving phone and Internet by satellite reliably and inexpensively seems to be in the future.

Let's assume your phone goes dead for some reason or another. What do you do? Either call the neighbors on a cell phone or run over to their place to determine if their service is out as well. The rule for rural folks is that the wider the area of service loss, the more likely the phone company will respond quickly, and with more people and equipment. If nothing else, knowing the scope of the problem and being able to report it to the phone company is helpful.

Mail and parcel delivery are an important part of rural communications. We maintain both an in-town postal box and a rural delivery mailbox. We could probably get by with the P.O. box only, but the rural delivery box has its advantages. It keeps our mail delivery person engaged with us, and as a result, she keeps a sharp watch when we are gone. Also, rural delivery boxes are tied to a physical address, which gives other delivery services such as UPS a target out in the country.

Don't expect rural delivery to be quite as fast and efficient as town delivery. I go out of my way to socialize with UPS, FedEx, and other delivery personnel, but I still get calls several times a year asking exactly who we are and where we live. It gets better after living in one place several years, yet we still can lose up to a day or two over delivery people not knowing how to get to our place. Seems the day we expect an important package is the day an alternate driver is on our route.

Rural carriers keep some stamps in their vehicles, and some might have limited ability to post small packages for patrons, but this service is falling into disuse. My grandparents used to place their package, along with a dollar or two, in the box. Next morning there was an envelope with change and a receipt. Today, rural carriers prefer that able-bodied people go to town to deal with their parcels personally. Most will post packages and letters only for shut-in elderly or infirm folks.

Here's a small bit of rural communications that is often overlooked. You will frequently find yourself giving out-of-towners instructions to get to your place. This routine often becomes more convoluted than it should be. You will find that city people race past tiny rural route signs on pitch-black roads (no streetlights out here), or they have no concept that a T-road is different from a crossroad. I have had my city friends drive 4 miles out of their way to a crossroad simply because they didn't recognize the branch of the T-road leading to our place! To overcome this problem, we drew up a detailed but simple map to our house and provide a photocopy to guests as needed.

I am reluctant to raise alarms about communications problems in the country, because rural life necessitates a degree of hardiness and self-sufficiency that should not be unduly tested by a few days of isolation. Nonetheless, rural newcomers should be aware that these situations exist and that dealing with them may not be as straightforward as they at first appear.

Chapter Seven

Energy

At least three locals really hate my guts. Out of county of approximately 29,000 and a state population of 1.2 million, this is probably acceptable.

All three are managers of regional liquid petroleum (LP) gas distributorships. They don't like me because I own my own 1,000-gallon LP gas tank. As a result, I can bargain fiercely over my annual purchase of LP gas. It would be far better for them if I would have taken their first offer and leased my storage tank. Then I would have had to accept whatever price was first quoted.

It's really a love/hate relationship. They can't ignore my annual 700- to 850-gallon purchase, allowing it to fall by default to a competitor. That I write out a check on the spot is another powerful incentive. At a savings of about $85 per year, it is sometimes questionable whether I will ever recover my original $1,600 lump sum payment for the tank. But there's more at play here than just saving money.

First, I don't want to have to pay the first price the gas company offers, and I don't want to be saddled with having to deal with only one gas company. Most of all, I don't want to risk having them come by to pick up the tank when they get a better offer or there is some sort of emergency.

Those are very good reasons for people to own their own fuel storage tanks, but the entire issue of energy in the country cuts a bit deeper than that. We are certainly not discussing a philosophy universally held by rural folks, but many experienced residents strongly believe that all people out in the country should have at least three separate sources of energy. We have four!

First of all, we have electricity pulled in from the grid. Standby generators assure that we will have at least some juice to perform tasks done best with electricity.

Second, we have a generous supply of firewood. I will have much more to say about using firewood as an energy source in Chapter 8.

Third, we store about 1,000 gallons of diesel oil on our property. This is fuel for the auxiliary home heater, tractors, and generator. Fourth is the LP gas storage. Our system is designed to provide back-up and redundancy. That way if the oil barrel goes dry, there is always firewood for the heat stove. During a really violent, howling storm, when getting to the woodpile is chancy, we can run the gas range burners, and so on.

LP gas and diesel heating oil have a few things in common. Both must be purchased well ahead of need, then be stored safely and conveniently on site for use throughout the year. I also recommend deploying two separate means of accessing this storage as a kind of ultimate redundancy. In our case, in addition to the underground feed lines from diesel oil tank to house, we have a hand-crank pump that can lift the oil into cans and barrels. The LP gas tank also has an external feed attached.

Many communities that once supported three or four fuel oil dealers are now down to one or less. Farmers and rural residents sometimes find they must bring in fuel oil from long distances. Newcomers to the country are wise to verify that all fuel sources are readily available in their area before planning to use them as part of a rural energy program.

Also be aware that, in many sections of the United States, including places with severe weather or harsh topography, delivery is not possible every day of the year. Delivery trucks are slow, clumsy, and often pretty helpless. Rain-swollen creeks, soft muddy roads, slick ice, and steep winding roads can easily preclude delivery. Top-heavy propane tank trucks are especially difficult and dangerous to maneuver over questionable roads. If access to your place is difficult, weeks might go by before some determined truck driver can get through.

As a working principle, we try to store heating oil and LP gas sufficient for one year's consumption. All deliveries can then be made in summer, when the grass is green and the birds are singing. Expense for this large inventory can be considerable even when factoring in how we bargain prices down a bit, but it agrees with our lifestyle quite well.

Purchasing and installing a 1,000-gallon underground fuel oil tank is relatively straightforward. Our first tar-coated, plain steel model was guaranteed for one year. It lasted 27 years. I took it out before any signs of failure to be certain it didn't start to leak. Would have been an expensive waste of oil, and any leakage could have threatened our water supply.

The modern option is to bury a 1,000-gallon, fiberglass-coated, heavy-gauge steel tank. These are guaranteed to last 35 years underground. Local petroleum products dealers can tell you who handles these tanks.

Inexpensive, tar-coated steel tanks are still available, but these are usually set on a special concrete pad within a small building that would also contain an accidental spill. Most spills occur when the tank is being filled and are relatively minor. Prices for plain steel tanks are less, but not when costs for a special building are also factored in.

Is it wise to bury a home fuel oil tank out of sight, away from possible damage and theft? Obviously I have concluded it is. For everyone else, it depends on rules, regulations, and circumstances. Some folks still use smaller oil tanks that they set in their garage or basement. These tanks can be smelly, unsightly, and cumbersome, always in the way of some project or expansion. Thousand-gallon tanks such as ours are far too large for garage or basement applications.

State regulations usually determine whether rural homeowners can bury fuel tanks on their property. Our state has an interest only in tanks of more than 1,000 gallons that are used for commercial purposes. Best check with local contractors, petroleum dealers, and home heating people before embarking on this journey.

A city engineer once gave me what is probably the best advice regarding burying a fuel tank. "Bed the tank in lots and lots of clean gravel," he advised. "The tank will last at least two to three times longer underground if you do." That's longer than I am going to live, so that's what I did with the last tank. A big $100 load of gravel did the trick nicely.

Purchasing and installing a large LP gas tank is tricky. Propane distributors are not dunces. Most recognize the fact that they lose their ability to hold captive customers who own their own tanks. Many refuse to sell propane tanks to anyone, especially larger sizes.

Whether leased or purchased, propane tanks blend poorly into the environment of all rural estates I can think of. Leased tanks are generally given a fresh coat of white paint every three or so years. Rather than leaving them sore-thumb white, those who own their own can paint their tanks whatever color they please. Many elect to paint them green, brown, or camouflage. Hiding the tank under military surplus camouflage netting is also effective. At any rate, keep the tank exterior clean, neat, and rust free with an occasional detergent wash and new coat of paint. No matter what the paint job, it's smart to locate the tank under cool shade trees, especially in hotter climates.

The most reasonable setup, I believe, is to place a camouflage-painted tank up on cement blocks and install external fittings and an extended fill hose. The fittings and hose dramatically increase the utility of the tank, allowing you to do things like refill an empty barbeque tank without having to lug it to town. Gravity, rather than a pump, does the work when filling small tanks from the nurse tank. Obviously, small tanks must be set below the level of the nurse tank when they're being filled, something that is impossible if the main tank is buried.

Special hoses and fittings used to fill 5- and 10-gallon "appliance" cylinders must be installed *before* the first gas fill on a new primary tank. Otherwise, residual gas that always remains in once-filled tanks will gush out, freezing the fingers while creating a potentially explosive situation.

When purchasing your supply of fuel, don't be hesitant to mention that the other dealer was 4 cents less per gallon and that even this seemed somewhat excessive. Also, I always ask if waiting till later in the summer will result in lower prices. Last year our heating oil dealer told me to wait, saying he would call when the price was right. We bought in September, saving about 5 cents per gallon.

Owning storage tanks for gas and oil may not be a great deal less expensive than leasing or using smaller, less expensive tanks, but self-sufficient rural folks find great comfort knowing that their year's supply of oil and gas is safely in the barn. Finding and purchasing storage tanks can be bewildering, but hopefully this brief introduction will shorten the trial and error period and make the experience less painful.

: Chapter Eight :

Firewood

Firewood, as both a source of fuel and aesthetics, is a more important issue than recent transplants to the country might first suppose. Fireplaces in rural homes are common, wood stoves for heating are almost ubiquitous, and there is always the issue of cleaning your grounds of woody debris, which becomes an asset when put in the stove.

Because newcomers to the country will almost certainly deal with firewood in one capacity or another, it is important for them to know how to evaluate quality and quantity of firewood as well as how it is produced, how tools for its production are used and maintained correctly, and how it is grown on the land as a renewable resource. This chapter will touch upon the major points, but check out Web sites like www.woodheat.org and www.firewood.com, which are clearinghouses for all sorts of useful firewood-related information.

Way back in the days on our farm, we used firewood both to heat the house and fuel our cook stove. There was nothing romantic or socially redeeming about the process. It was hard work, requiring more skill than modern folks would ever suppose. We did it because that's what we did. We didn't know any different.

Gathering firewood back then was dangerous. Equipment such as the large, unprotected circular saw we used to cut logs was so threatening, just thinking about it today is painful!

Like most farmsteads during that era, ours had an active, managed woodlot. Clearing trees from the lot provided ground that we eventually farmed or used for pasture for our horses and cattle. Starting as close to the house as possible, we fenced off a 20-acre section of trees and underbrush. Into this closure we drove a great many cattle and whatever else we had that would eat the vegetation. Soon the thundering herd's continual browsing, trampling, and chewing killed all the underbrush and many of the trees.

Just as soon as the ground dried but before fieldwork commenced, we chopped down the dead trees. With the brush gone, it was relatively easy to use a horse team to haul the logs to an area near the woodshed where the saw was set up. (Folks today seem more shocked to learn that there really were such things as woodsheds rather than that nine-year-old boys helped run big, dangerous, whirring circular saws.)

Regardless of the wood's character, we cut all the logs into sections called rounds. These were split and stacked in the woodshed to dry for a year. Good and dense or light and punky—all the wood eventually went into the stoves. Clearing land, getting rid of debris, and heating and cooking were equally important to us, so we used it all.

Today, even folks who plan to burn only modest amounts of wood as a supplement to their main heating fuel can save large amounts of cash by doing so. As we did with our old woodlot, modern rural dwellers can clean up, maintain, and manage their tree-covered acreage. They don't have to do it by fencing, grazing, and clearing but by simple, wise use of an available resource.

But all wood is not created equal. Management of both woodlot and firebox requires some knowledge of species and conventions of the trade. This is true whether you make firewood yourself or purchase it from a dealer.

A cord of hickory firewood, for instance, has the heating equivalent of more than 200 gallons of fuel oil! Even after deducting a 50 percent efficiency loss for the average, old-fashioned wood stove, you still come out ahead. Newer catalytic models of stoves are often 75 percent efficient or better. These modern units are also fairly expensive, so don't throw out the old stove that came with the place right away!

The benefits of producing your own firewood from what's available on your property are remarkable. The wood is free for the cutting, splitting, and hauling. Removing it tidies your land while cutting down on fire danger. You save money by not having to pay taxes on store-bought fuel. And, of course, trees for firewood are a renewable resource. There are, however, a few other economic considerations that are not immediately obvious to rural neophytes.

Knowing which tree species provide the most bang for your buck is important. Woodcutters know that light basswood or pine contains less heat value per cord than white oak, but few of them understand that it's about half. Basswood and pine have heating oil equivalence of approximately 36 gallons per cord in standard-efficiency wood-burning stoves; white oak has as much heat value as 65 gallons of fuel oil. In some cases it might not even pay to make up basswood or pine to haul home for the wood furnace. In the case of really light woods such as willow or cedar, one could easily lose money even when factoring in free labor. Better to spend time "working up" hickory tops and other energy-rich debris into stove wood, especially if it is abundant and close at hand or is otherwise creating a messy fire hazard out on the estate.

Whether making up their own or buying from a firewood supplier, the chart on page 73 demonstrates that frugal users are well-advised to identify the best heating species available in their area and to be cautious regarding how much they pay per cord or, in the case of making firewood, which species they spend time and money gathering.

Learning to identify various species of trees can be a chore or a delight, depending on one's perspective. But whether you enjoy it or not, you will have to learn this skill, and here's another reason why: firewood sellers are notorious for offering loads of mixed species. Beware—these can be bad bargains.

Conventional firewood wisdom claims that heavier wood always contains more energy. Long-lived, slow-growing trees with many closely spaced annual growth rings per inch are usually heavier and denser. Wise firewood buyers look for density as well as species when possible.

Firewood is traded on a unit volume measure called a cord. A cord of wood is defined as a neat stack measuring 4 feet wide, 4 feet high, and 8 feet long. Rural convention dictates that this stack of wood must be split and piled sufficiently close that a tree squirrel could find a few pathways through which to pass, but a pursuing cat could not follow. To put it a little more precisely, woodcutters reckon that a cord, even when tightly packed, should contain about 85 cubic feet of solids, about a third less than the 128 cubic feet in a proper 4 x 4 x 8 foot pile of split wood.

As a result of these imprecise measurements involving fleeing squirrels and pursuing cats, you might encounter some strange jargon buying firewood. You might hear volumes of wood described as face cords, pickup cords, stove cords, or—my all-time favorite—a "fitted cord" (whatever that is). Never mind all that. They all have one thing in common—they describe a pile of wood having considerably less than 128 cubic feet.

There are two ways, then, for city slickers to be swindled by rural firewood sellers: they receive wood of inferior or mixed species, or they receive less than a true cord measure. Unless prices are adjusted dramatically lower, these "cords" tend not to be good values. As a fallback, use the chart on page 73 to purchase firewood by weight rather than volume.

City transplants who want to save money on heating by cleaning up around the estate or occasionally enjoying an aesthetic fire are going to have to know something about chain saws. Not all rural homeowners have chain saws, but most eventually find it convenient to own at least one.

I don't believe a chain saw is any more dangerous than a big power hand saw, but accidents do occur among amateur users. Some jurisdictions even require new chain saw owners to take practical application safety courses before they can take delivery of a new saw. Follow a few simple safety rules and the risks of chain saw use become negligible:

- Neophytes should purchase a medium-sized saw with short to intermediate length bar (i.e., the saw's cutting edge). Trying to learn on a big, powerful, 50cc saw with 28-inch bar would be a mistake.
- Always wear heavy work boots, thick canvas pants, a good face shield, and sound-deadening earmuffs when cutting with the saw.
- No one else should be allowed within 6 feet of the operating saw.
- Never reach up above eye level with the saw.
- Nothing except wood should ever touch the bar.

Heat Recovery of Various Wood Species compared with Fuel Oil*

Species	Density at 20% Moisture Content in Pounds/cu.ft.	Average Weight of 85 cu.ft. @ 20% moisture content in pounds Equals one cord load of solid wood	Possible Recoverable Heat Units per cord of 85 solid cu.ft. at 100% efficiency and 20% moisture content in millions of BTUs	Available heat per cord at 50% heating efficiency provided by most wood stoves in millions of BTUs	Equivalent gallons of fuel oil @ 60% burning efficiency for oil furnace
Hickory	50.9	4,327	27.7	13.8	70.6
Eastern Ironwood	50.2	4,267	27.3	13.7	69.6
Apple	48.7	4,140	26.5	13.2	67.5
White Oak	47.2	4,012	25.7	12.8	65.4
Sugar Maple	44.2	3,757	24.0	12.0	61.2
Red Oak	44.2	3,757	24.0	12.0	61.2
Beech	44.2	3,757	24.0	12.0	61.2
Yellow Birch	43.4	3,689	23.6	11.8	60.2
White Ash	43.4	3,689	23.6	11.8	60.2
Hackberry	38.2	3,247	20.8	10.4	53.1
Tamarack	38.2	3,247	20.8	10.4	53.1
Paper Birch	37.4	3,179	20.3	10.2	51.8
Red Fir	34.9	3,155	22.3	11.1	56.8
Cherry	36.7	3,120	20.0	10.0	51.0
Elm	35.9	3,052	19.5	9.8	49.7
Black Ash	35.2	2,992	19.1	9.6	48.7
Red (Soft) Maple	34.4	2,924	18.7	9.4	47.7
Box Elder	32.9	2,797	17.9	8.9	45.5
Jack Pine	31.4	2,669	17.1	8.5	43.5
Norway Pine	31.4	2,669	17.1	8.5	43.5
Lodgepole Pine	30.7	2,610	17.5	8.8	44.6
Hemlock	29.2	2,482	15.9	7.9	40.4
Black Spruce	29.2	2,482	15.9	7.9	40.4
Aspen	27.0	2,295	14.7	7.3	37.4
White Pine	26.3	2,236	14.3	7.2	36.5
Balsam Fir	26.3	2,236	14.3	7.2	36.5
Grans Fir	25.4	2,160	16.7	8.4	42.6
Cottonwood	24.8	2,108	13.5	6.7	34.3
Basswood	24.8	2,108	13.5	6.7	34.3
Northern White Cedar	22.5	1,913	12.2	6.1	31.1

*Chart Compiled from information provided by the University of Minnesota and the University of Idaho

- Do not poke or punch the end of the bar into a log or the ground. Professionals who inadvertently dig their bars into the ground immediately stop and sharpen the saw.

It is also an excellent rule of thumb that rural neophytes with woodcutting chores should purchase a relatively expensive chain saw. Stihl, Jonsered, or Husqvarna are really the only ones to consider. More firewood can be produced with less maintenance and irritating breakdowns using this grade of professional equipment.

The big difference between expensive and cheap chain saws occurs when tallying variable costs for wear and consumptive items such as gasoline and oil (which cost more on cheaper saws because they consume more), new chains and bars, clutches, sprockets, air cleaners, and other spare parts. You must also factor in high labor costs on cheaper models with frequent breakdowns when repairs can't be made at home.

Professional model saws require about half a gallon of gasoline, 4 ounces of two-cycle oil, and 8 ounces of bar lubricating oil per cord of finished firewood. Five miles haulage from up on the mountain to our house in our old, beater truck consumes another gallon of gasoline. Easy math suggests that the 12 cords of firewood I burn annually requires less than 20 gallons of gasoline and a gallon and a half of oil. (As an aside, electric chain saws are completely out of the equation. Nobody seriously considers them capable of handling much practical work.)

Even at their best, chain saws are complex tools, often difficult for inexperienced owners to keep in top running condition. Properly sharpening a chain, for instance, can be a daunting task for a neophyte. Unfortunately, sharpening is a common maintenance task, often done after each fill of the fuel tank and lubricating reservoir.

Here is the quick, easy, efficient method of learning how to maintain a chain saw, including sharpening the chain. Don't be disappointed if learning to do this job correctly takes a few years along with some practical coaching from an experienced hand.

First, as mentioned previously, purchase a rugged, more forgiving professional saw. Some beginners purchase used saws, cheaper models of saws, or very small, limited-capacity "learner saws" in hopes these tools will provide good learning opportunities. That's okay, but expect increased expense and frustration, especially when the saws are kept running over long periods of time.

Second, at the repair/sales shop, explain that this is your first chain saw purchase and that, if it's a used or smaller one, you intend to purchase a full-size model as soon as you are comfortable operating one. Ask if it would be possible to watch and learn whenever you bring it in for repairs. Include sharpening the chain in this request.

Offering to purchase a new saw at the end of the learning session is usually sufficient incentive for most shops to agree to your proposal. You are still paying for repairs; you just want to watch them being made. If the dealer won't allow it, look elsewhere for a smaller, friendlier shop. This is not an unusual request in rural areas. Of the five saw shops I have dealt with during my lifetime, only one refused this deal.

Chain sharpening is not particularly easy or intuitive. If it's done poorly, wood cutting becomes slow and laborious, and the chain may wear prematurely. Expect your first few chains to wear faster than necessary due to your amateur bungling with the file. But with patience, experience, and the following tips, you can do it yourself.

Proceed by tightening the chain till it can just be pulled out about an inch to an inch and a half from the guide bar. Loose chains cut poorly until they finally jump off the bar and must be reinstalled. Longer bars and chains are more subject to stretching. As with sharpening, retightening the chain is usually done whenever you refuel.

Acquire the correct-size files for your chain as well as a stamped steel guide for the job. This guide will keep the file at the correct depth on the teeth and demonstrate via markings the correct angle at which to cut. Chains sharpened at the wrong angle and depth dull quickly.

Basically, correctly filing a chain involves *always* cutting from the inside out. Never file in both directions, and never file teeth on both sides of the chain simultaneously. Saw chains are put together with teeth spaced every 3 inches or so along the chain. The teeth point toward the outside in an alternating pattern. (This is not so confusing when actually looking at a chain.)

Sharpen all the teeth on one side, filing to the outside only. You know all is well when the file makes a nice, dull, even cutting sound as it pushes through. When angle and depth are wrong, the cut produces more of a shrill, screeching sound. After filing all the teeth on one side, turn the saw around and file the teeth on the other side. Again, cut only in one direction.

You can find chain saw files for as little as $2 each. They are good for perhaps five sharpenings before wearing out. Life and efficiency of a file can be extended a bit by tapping out the fine metal shavings every stroke or two. Also, turn the file very slightly in the holder every so often. This exposes a new set of teeth while allowing neighboring teeth to empty of their metal shavings.

Do not endure a loose, dull chain, even though sharpening one can be bewildering initially. Again, ask your dealer for help with proper technique. Many dealers use power tools to sharpen shop saws, but they all know how to use a hand file correctly. You could invest in a power sharpener of your own if you think you'll be cutting enough wood (12-volt models go for as little as $20; larger 110- and 120-volt bench-mount sharpeners are in the $200–$400 range), or do as some pros do and bring three or four chains to the woods with you so there's no downtime sharpening during a big job.

Some well-meaning rural folks never cut a tree on their property. That's their decision, but other people see trees as a crop, just like corn or wheat. All depends on your own beliefs and circumstances.

All trees mature and die. Somebody or something will fell them eventually. Storm damage, insects, and disease will take their toll, especially on unmanaged trees. In my case, a tree dies, I clean it up. With less competition, those next to it begin a growth spurt. As my harvested trees disappear into the stove, those remaining expand out into the space available. Managed wisely, it really becomes a renewable and sustainable energy source.

Chapter Nine

Gardens and Rural Greenery

Our Southern-raised daughter-in-law enjoys cooking with okra and eggplant, so raising her own garden-fresh okra and eggplant is a high priority for her. Unfortunately, it is one that has completely eluded her to date. Since leaving the South, she has never lived in a place where these vegetables are raised without agricultural heroics. Raising exotics in her current location is possible, but it is sufficiently difficult that her need is more easily satisfied shopping in the produce section of her local supermarket.

Lush gardens, productive fruit trees, and great green lawns are a top priority for many folks looking at a move to the country. If you are one of these people, your move should also include a realistic gauge of your personal skill and determination.

In my experience, it takes from three to five years to learn to manage a successful but otherwise common garden in a new area. Some idea of what can be commonly grown can be gleaned from local residents or from garden shops, but two cautions should be observed.

First, keep in mind that gardening neighbors may be experts at coaxing things out of the soil after years of experimentation. By all means talk to them and gain from their experience, but know that you are probably going to have to go through your own trial-and-error phase before reaching their level of competence.

Second, it is often difficult to determine ahead of time which of even common garden vegetables and fruit trees will do well on the specific piece of ground you have in mind. For example, consider the fact that thousands of wild, untended apple trees dot the countryside around my home. Most produce scraggly, insignificant fruit of little joy to eaters other than deer. Early Johnny Appleseed settlers spotted these trees about in an attempt to determine where apples did especially well in the region. Today some of these trees remain, aged and broken, but they are still here. The point is that apples grow over a wide area hereabouts, but they do not grow *well* everyplace.

Some soils can be built, altered, and manipulated to accommodate fruits and vegetables that would not normally do well there. Rhubarb is a good local example. Like most Midwestern transplants, we love the stuff! Stewed and in pies, we judge it all good. But rhubarb requires soils with as neutral pH as possible. Due to the fact that we know about this idiosyncrasy, we spread inexpensive lime on our rhubarb patches. As a result, we raise lots of rhubarb even when our neighbors' untended plants wither and die.

Unless gardening is very important to you, you probably won't purchase rural property on the basis of soil composition. If gardening *is* a big part of your plan for your new life in the country, get a soil test before purchasing a hunk of land. Virtually every rural community has a local soil-testing service that will evaluate for nutrient and pH levels, soil particle size composition, and other factors vital to healthy, productive growth. A $100 test will tell the entire tale.

Next, check out exact climate data for your intended area and apply it to your garden and lawn requirements. What are the frost-free dates, average monthly highs and lows, and precipitation levels? Some of this information is available from the U.S. Department of Agriculture's plant hardiness zone maps (available on the web at http://www.usna.usda.gov/Hardzone/ushzmap.html). Incredibly detailed and accurate documents, these maps plot average minimum temperatures state by state down to the county level.

Finally, talk to gardening neighbors and the helpful staff at the local nursery. Find out about the idiosyncrasies of the soil as well as the tricks they use to battle damaging critters, insects, and weather. If you have moved to an agricultural region, ask what agronomic technology is used to manage soil, deal with disease and pests, and increase the quality and quantity of crop output.

This discussion will bring you face-to-face with what has become a heated topic in modern rural communities—chemicals. The recent influx of non-agricultural residents to the countryside has clouded issues of chemical use there. Many newcomers fear these tools, thinking incorrectly that they will turn the tap water to churning poison or elevate cancer rates in the region. Likewise, they don't realize the unintended consequences of an anti-chemical stance when it comes to things like low soil fertility (requiring high inputs of chemical fertilizers), pest infestations (requiring high inputs of insecticides), and weed control (requiring high inputs of herbicides, as it is often a landowner's legal responsibility to control noxious weeds on his property before they spread and damage other people's crops).

An acquaintance who once worked for the U.S. State Department in Bangkok, Thailand, once noted that only people who have never stood out in the blazing hot sun amidst an ocean-like field chopping weeds by hand for 12 hours a day are anti-herbicide. Similarly, my experience has been that whenever aphids start decimating one's own cherry trees, notions of chemical prohibitions are quickly and conveniently forgotten.

It is not true that long-term rural people, especially farmers, needlessly and dangerously scatter these materials at random over their property. Economic considerations alone preclude that approach. On the other hand, other economic considerations are currently producing a generation of organic farmers. In their constant search for more profitable enterprises, many American farmers are becoming born-again organics.

This is not to suggest that, by some quirk of fate or sudden insight, these people have seen the error of their ways. Rather, in many instances this type of farming has simply become identified as a trendy, perhaps temporary niche from which they can turn a profit.

Raising and marketing organic beans, lettuce, peas, tomatoes, or artichokes may be a business decision devoid of any other philosophical underpinnings. An organic entrepreneur may have a chemical-free commercial field crop, while his bright, hurt-your-eyes-green front lawn may be the result of the 100 pounds of pure urea fertilizer he applies each fall. Wise city slickers keep this possibility in mind before making assumptions about other people's choices.

All of this flows back to the truth that when it's your own Douglas firs the tussock moths are stripping, or your pond that is breeding clouds of mosquitoes, or your home being chomped by carpenter ants or termites, it is much more difficult to be anti-chemical. If it's great fields of crops and next year's entire income, it's virtually impossible to maintain purity on the issue of chemical use. Modern farmers not engaged in specialty organic production are not fearful of agricultural chemicals for a couple of significant reasons. First, modern pesticides, herbicides, and fertilizers are tested extensively before being approved for distribution and use. Today's litigious society demands nothing less. All these materials have been subjected to a litany of tests to determine that no discernible residues remain and that any that do are benign.

Second, other than certain fertilizer applications, modern agricultural chemicals are actually used in relatively low quantities. They are too expensive to "slather" on fields, as some media people glibly suggest. Most farmers do not have extra money for "slathering" anything! As a result, they apply their materials in a more even, consistent, and diluted fashion than your typical landowner trying to coax a large garden, lawn, or orchard out of their own parcel.

Scientific research and technological innovation have traditionally been an integral part of rural America, resulting in a demonstrably better way of life not only for the farmers who produce the world's food supply but the billions of people who receive it. This betterment includes long-lasting farm machinery; inexpensive veterinary supplies; fast-growing, feed-efficient livestock; efficient, user-friendly pesticides and fertilizers; GPS-directed planting, watering, and fertilizing systems; instant electronic marketing information; and enough other remarkable improvements to fill several pages.

At this moment, biotechnology is delivering on some preliminary promises of new plant varieties that are resistant to age-old depredations from insects and disease. American farmers classify biotech as another form of selective breeding. As a result, don't expect any new technology that reduces expense, uncertainty, and wear and tear dragging equipment across a field while dramatically increasing yields to be ignored by farmers competing in a free market.

My earnest suggestion is for newcomers to wait at least three to four years before making up their minds on these issues or taking strong public stands on them. Established rural folks have a number of good reasons for using agricultural chemicals and for not being fearful of ag-biotech. This does not make them disdainful or disrespectful of the good earth. They've lived very close to it for generations, so they are fully aware of the need to treat it correctly and carefully. Doing otherwise would only endanger their livelihood, their family's financial future, and their very way of life.

A final word on one of the wonderful hallmarks of country living: trees. Living among tall trees is an aesthetic treat for most people. We used to throw our bedrolls out under the trees at night and fall asleep under the rustling leaves. Yet trees can be a mixed blessing. In parts of the West, Douglas fir and Ponderosa pines shed huge amounts of fine pollen every spring. Clouds of nasty yellow dust blow through every time the wind comes up. Pollen accumulates as thick dust on decks, houses, and vehicles. It doesn't usually last more than a week or two early, but newcomers are often taken by surprise by the misery this stuff creates.

Those especially bothered by pollen or who experience allergies can install central air conditioning with sophisticated electronic filters. Prescriptions are available to battle hay fever that are much more effective—and expensive—than over-the-counter remedies. But was this additional trouble and expense calculated into initial purchase decisions? More important, will this unanticipated hassle lead to total dissatisfaction with country life?

My guess is probably not, but once again, it's something you need to factor in to your decision-making process before making a significant investment in a new home in the country.

Chapter Ten

Your Own Pond

Few things epitomize the delight and ambiance of rural life better than owning and enjoying a small, private pond of your very own. Kids delight in a safe, convenient place in which to piddle around, catching a giant catfish or unwary bullfrog. Adults find solace in watching the kids play, swim, or fish or in just sitting near the cool water and relaxing. Ducks land, deer come to drink, and critters great and small quickly make a new pond a stopping place in their journeys.

Given minimal space and topographical requirements, ponds are not particularly difficult to construct. Maintenance can also be extremely simple. We mow around our pond twice a year and unplug the overflow drainpipe every spring. That's it. The grandkids catch all the fish!

Initial construction costs, given a bit of luck locating a proper site, can be modest—from a half to a third the cost of a new car in most cases. Lower fire insurance rates, plus the peace of mind knowing one has an alternate water source in an emergency, may lighten the financial burden. About the only special financial consideration might be the liability issue if your manmade body of water were to be cited as an "attractive nuisance" should a neighbor's kid drowns in it while you are away.

Wildlife-specific ponds are built somewhat differently than swimming or fishing ponds. If attracting, observing, and assisting wildlife are the pond's primary functions, construct it in or near a forest. Trees and brush provide protective refuge for shy animals. But there are always tradeoffs: ducks and geese may not use the pond because of their fear of birds of prey that lurk in tall surrounding trees. Small nocturnal mammals such as raccoons, fox, possums, and mink will be attracted no matter where the pond is built, whether it's in a little draw way out in a bare field or right in front of the house.

Water-dwelling critters, including muskrat and beaver, may eventually proliferate to the point where control measures must be deployed. Pond owners, in their desire to provide nice living conditions for animals, must stay in touch with reality, helping only to the extent that the pond's original purpose is maintained. Sometimes this is difficult. An abundance of semi-wild Canada geese, for instance, produces conditions that are less than desirable for swimmers. Too many burrowing muskrats may breach the dam.

According to the Natural Resources Conservation Service (NRCS, formerly the U.S. Soil Conservation Service)—a federal agency that does most of the preliminary engineering on new ponds in the United States—large areas are not required for successful private ponds. Most private ponds, no matter what their original purpose, fall into the one-half to two-and-a-half acre range. Takes only a dab of what is often thought to be waste or unproductive property to put one in.

Again, original purpose drives engineering. Necessary depth depends entirely on one's climate zone and the planned use of the finished product. Ice-skating, for instance, is safer on a shallow pond, but such a pond is only practical north of the Mason/Dixon line. Shallow, regular-shaped ponds are easier to clean out and maintain. On the other end of the spectrum, trout require deeper, cooler ponds. Catfish will grow and fatten in ponds no more than 3 to 5 feet deep should owners be faced with that limitation or especially prefer catfish. Shallow southern ponds that freeze with only a skin of ice will support catfish. Farther north, shallow ponds may freeze deep enough to kill all the fish. Fishing ponds generally need only be dug 10 to 12 feet deep, no matter where in the United States they are located.

The good folks at the NRCS (www.nrcs.usda.gov) can give you advice regarding specific considerations for your area. These helpful, knowledgeable people usually have an office in the county courthouse or regional federal building. Also check with your state Department of Fish and Game conservation officer for good, local information. In the course of their analyses, these people will look for sufficient runoff, suitable topsoil and subsoils, and optimal wildlife and recreation situations. They are also sources for cost-effective, proven construction techniques.

Pond location, NRCS experts point out, is not nearly as critical as one might suspect. Running streams or free-flowing springs are not necessary and may actually constitute a red-tape permit obstacle. One local city transplant wanted a pond in front of his home, and he also wanted his home built out on a bare ridge with a drop-dead view. The fellow drilled an extra well from which he pumps water into the pond—another instance of sufficient money overcoming all obstacles.

Better to look for more natural locations. Water runoff down a broad gully or draw or from an extended hillside is usually more than sufficient to fill a pond. Ponds surrounded by grassy, woody brush generally require far less maintenance than their cousins surrounded by farmed fields. Silt, chemical residue, and fertilizer-laden runoff from farmed fields as well, as erosion caused by access roads surrounding new ponds, may dump materials that cause algae to bloom and benefit choking weeds and grasses. Without grass and brush to catch runoff-borne materials, new ponds may silt and vegetate in in as little as six to eight years. It's not the end of the pond, but it costs money to have a contractor called in to redredge or to do it yourself.

NRCS people know all this. Applying their extensive training and experience, they will survey the area and recommend dam height, construction methods, and materials. They will set flags for fill location lines, the dam, and the spillway. They take deep core soil samples to ascertain presence or absence of clay layers needed to seal a pond properly. They also note extent and condition of gravel layers which, if extensive, could cause the pond to leak and drain. Dump truck loads of slick sealing clay can be hauled in to paste up a leaking pond under virtually any adverse condition, but, again, expenses increase. Liquid polymers that are added to the water and allowed to seep into the soil and seal it are also available. In any case, it's far better to know what one is getting into before having to rely on these methods to seal a leaking pond.

Government permits, which must be obtained prior to construction, vary widely from state to state. Some states allow rural landowners to build without permits, provided the pond's dam is less than 10 to 12 feet high and total pond size is less than an acre or two. NRCS officials have up-to-date information regarding permits as well as the names of key people in the regulatory agencies.

In years past, NRCS funds were available as a means of government encouragement of and cost sharing for rural pond building. Although this program has passed into oblivion, farmers having a business purpose for their ponds can depreciate construction expenses. Unfortunately, rural neophytes interested in providing aesthetics or fire protection find no tax benefit at the hard-hearted IRS.

Locating an experienced, reliable pond builder often starts at the NRCS office. They have lists of contractors and heavy equipment operators who grub out ponds and construct dams. Call these, plus any other earth-moving operators in the area. Yellow Pages listings, general contractors, and other pond owners can usually provide leads. Often it's a case of, "I don't do that, but old Preston Jones in Uniontown does." Go see Jones if his name comes up. The goal is to find a heavy equipment operator who has constructed a minimum of 10 ponds in the area during fairly recent times. Nothing replaces current experience in the pond-building business.

When you talk to pond owners, remember that price is not the only issue. Determine how neat and orderly the work was performed. Did they tear up little trees on land surrounding the pond? Was precious topsoil buried under yards of barren subsoil? Ask if the pond held water from the get-go or if it had to be sealed with clay or liquid polymer later. Was the dam properly surveyed and packed? Sloppy dam survey work will allow spring runoff to overtop it in the wrong place, perhaps threatening the entire structure.

Most important, determine if the contractor has enough experience to adapt and engineer as he works. An adaptive mentality is extremely important when building ponds. Even if you are willing to undertake costly, detailed engineering, there will be minor surprises as the pond comes together. Nobody really knows exactly what lies 6 feet underground. Experienced heavy equipment operators gain their reputation by knowing how to cope with unexpected circumstances.

NRCS engineers will have rough cost estimates based on their drawings and soil samples as well as past experience in your area. Contractors may, in part, use these estimates, or they may use their own historic earth-moving costs to determine a finished price. From one third to a half down is customary, paid at the time an agreement is reached.

Construction can and should proceed quickly. Plan to have everybody on hand when the trucks and bulldozers pull in. It's really a grand show.

Ponds built in low areas that also contain active moving water must be built quickly lest they fill before work is completed. Ponds are usually dug only during the driest months of the year, but unplanned rain can quickly spoil those efforts. Contractors with insufficiently large equipment or who needlessly dilly-dally can find themselves in a huge mess. Another thing to ask the references.

Pond building commences by scraping all surplus surface trees and brush into a pile. Topsoil should be collected into another pile for later use as a covering for edges and dam face. Stabilizing grasses are eventually sown in this soil. Trees at or near the waterline are frequently removed—either they will die in a year or two, creating removal problems, or they may shed unwanted leaves and debris into the pond. Brushy piles are burned after they dry out. In the interim, noxious weeds in the piles must be controlled.

Clay subsoil—*not* containing stumps, large rocks, and miscellaneous material that will cause the dam to leak if used during construction—is piled into a line comprising the base of the new dam, and the heavy equipment packs everything into a solid, cohesive mass. Gradually a hole emerges from the muddy, sticky chaos. Ideally, the finished hole should be lined with a tight, water-resistant layer of packed clay or subsoil.

In states where dam height is closely regulated, contractors may dig a much deeper hole back in the center of the pond area or even into the draw where the pond is located. Legal dam heights are thus maintained while depths necessary to maintain fish are achieved without violating rules or necessitating sometimes difficult-to-obtain permits.

Heavy equipment contractors, other pond owners, and even swimming pool owners will be aware of evaporation rates in the area. These rates give some indication of the rise and fall of pond levels throughout the year. This data also assists NRCS specialists in predicting the time it will take for the pond to fill and the intensity of runoff over the spillway. Your pond's viability as a fishing hole will be determined by how low the water falls during the dry season.

Excess water flows out of the pond into either a spillway over the dam or through an overflow pipe laid beneath the dam at the start of construction. Overflow pipes beneath the dam are more costly to install and are potentially more difficult to maintain. High pressures at the foot of the dam tend to force water around the outside of the pipe, breaking down the dam and eventually washing it out. More expensive construction methods can be used to minimize this problem. On the other hand, when the pipe is opened fully, sediment in the bottom of the pond is washed out. For this reason, more complicated and expensive bottom discharge systems are sometimes favored over spillways by rural pond owners.

Owners of small, recreational ponds may be perfectly content with spillways cut into the top of the dam and lined with grass, rock, and plastic. Not only is this system less expensive to build, it is easier to maintain than pipes submerged 10 to 12 feet beneath the water.

Sometimes the hardest part of the project is waiting for the pond to fill. This is an excellent time to seed all recently scarred ground with stabilizing grasses. Decisions can also be made regarding the pond's habitat.

Some folks are trout people. Others favor a bluegill/bass economy. Still others prefer catfish because of the large sizes they eventually reach. More tightly balanced combinations such as catfish on the bottom, bluegills and bass in the middle, and bullfrogs on the banks are possible. Some species will gradually die out because they cannot propagate naturally. Others will outproduce everyone's fishing efforts. Non-breeder species must be stocked anew, while overly prolific types must be trapped, netted, or poisoned to control them. Local Fish and Game personnel can assist with predictions and information on what might thrive and what won't in your pond.

Some state Fish and Game departments offer free fish-stocking programs for new pond owners. Doesn't hurt to ask, but be sure to determine that free stocking does not then entitle the public to fish your pond, which is the case in some states. If Fish and Game does not offer this program in your area, they usually know of vendors who sell stockable fish and frogs. Private vendors are also good sources of information on species and stocking rates. Ask around, keeping in mind that conflicting information is usually related to the desire on somebody's part to sell you more fish.

Most new pond owners elect to stock a few large, almost mature, fish of each species. These are immediately catchable and are a bit more able to avoid mink, herons, and raccoons that sometimes seriously depredate young fish. Older, larger fish are a pain to transport safely, but they do start reproducing sooner, effectively jump-starting the pond fishing program.

After a year or two, it is virtually impossible to overfish a pond. Even very young children can safely spend hour after hour trying to entice a fish to take their bait, or they can play blissfully in the shallow end pursuing frogs and turtles.

Most rural people find ponds to be a wonderful family investment. Whether it's used for fishing, swimming, boating, ice-skating, wildlife viewing, or just tranquil relaxation, a private pond provides activities and moments that are pure gold. It's one of the few instances in life where dreams really do match reality.

Chapter Eleven

Tractors and Involuntary Servitude

Some counterculture types who take up rural residence see a spiritual component to hard labor. They embrace the ethic of physical work to the point where they actively seek old, even primitive means to accomplish the many, many chores that come with running a home and patch of land in the country. "It's okay," they tell themselves, "because we are doing the right thing for all of humanity." Who can argue against being at peace with yourself and humanity?

My experience strongly suggests that far more people move to the country to dramatically *improve* their living standard and quality of life, not to flee running water, lawn mowers, thermostats, laundry appliances, and other modern conveniences. If you are one of these people, I have one piece of advice: *buy a tractor.* Without a tractor, your rural paradise is in danger of becoming a dump or a slave labor camp rather than a pleasant retreat. Those who heed this recommendation will enjoy their rural experience a great deal more.

The practical value of tractor ownership cannot be overstated. With a compact but sturdy tractor, you won't have to spend precious hours mowing grass, splitting wood, cutting fire lanes, or cultivating a garden. Tractor manufacturers recognize this and have jumped into the small, rugged tractor business, producing powerful, multipurpose models ideally suited for rural estates. New Holland, Kubota, and John Deere are the three principal manufacturers. There are also models from China, Russia, and South Korea, and some of these less expensive imports are excellent values.

Having owned several tractors large and small in my lifetime, I have developed strong opinions on what I consider to be their must-have features. Anyone with an eye on cutting rural labor to manageable levels has to apply what I refer to as my list of "gottas" to tractor purchase—things you gotta have on small tractors.

First, purchase a sturdy four-wheel-drive model. Many new tractor owners purchase too small a machine, usually because they underestimate how handy and useful a tractor really can be. Don't be one of them. Determine the horsepower size both you and the dealer believe will be appropriate for your specific application, then purchase *at least* the next size larger.

Second: Look at tractors that have a power take-off (PTO) capacity. PTO shafts transfer power from the tractor to run all sorts of equipment, including lawn mowers, snow blowers, cement mixers, and a wide range of farm devices. Newbie landowners, perhaps intimidated by the notion of owning and operating a tractor, frequently end up purchasing a number of specialized machines: a big ride-on lawn mower, power lawn sweeper, stand-alone log splitter, self-contained motorized generator, walk-behind rototiller, gasoline-powered sprayer, and a rock-and log-hauling ATV.

Big mistake! Doing so leaves one a bunch of expensive, probably light-duty machines that never do the job as fast or as well as bigger, heavier equipment. Upfront costs for all these devices are considerable, and the various maintenance requirements for each become chores in themselves. Numerous makes and models of compact tractors are available that, when paired with PTO capacity and appropriate tools, handle all these rural tasks, plus scores more.

Third: Look for a universal three-point hitch capability. These sturdy hitches enable you to attach a tremendous array of chore-performing power tools to your tractor simply by slipping three pins into holes. Takes a minute or two when done on a level surface.

Finally, make sure your machine has a sturdy hydraulic capacity. Tractors equipped with hydraulics lift things by pumping oil into hydraulic cylinders. Pushing one lever lifts a heavy load of gravel or digs a deep hole, saving incredible wear and tear on back muscles. Believe me, it's much easier than trying to do the work with chain hoists, pry bars, block and tackle assemblies, and similar gear.

Not every tractor job will require hydraulics, a three-point hitch, and power take-off capability. But tractors that have them will be able to perform a number of chores and utilize a tremendous array of implements.

But beware. Some tractors have unique mounting systems for accessories and implements rather than accommodating an industry-wide standard. The popular low-clearance Bobcat tractors are an example. These machines will accommodate several different tools, but the mounting is peculiar to Bobcat. If forces you to purchase Bobcat-produced—and relatively expensive—tools.

Few rural homeowners can predict exactly which jobs they will wish to automate in the future. Grass mowing and snow removal are givens, but what about lawn seeding, tree planting, or barn cleaning when you still don't own a barn? Those with a versatile, properly equipped tractor don't have to predict their future needs because they'll already have their options covered. With a tractor, one can acquire tools and implements as needed. As compared to stand-alone, single-purpose machines, tractor tools are much less expensive and much more long-lived and sturdy. Additionally, it is not uncommon for rural neighbors to trade or loan tractor tools. You don't have to buy one until you are certain of the ongoing need.

The list of tools available for your tractor goes on and on. Glance at an implement dealer's catalog or Web site and you will be amazed. There are grass mowers, mulching machines, brush cutters, wood chippers, lawn vacuums, winches, fertilizer spreaders, irrigation and fire suppression pumps, sprayers, graders, plows, post hole diggers, generators, trenching machines, cement mixers, log splitters, backhoes, and dozens more I haven't thought of, have never needed, and perhaps have never even seen.

One rule of successful automated tool acquisition is to purchase only big, rugged implements intended for commercial applications. These are the ones with the capacity to get jobs done quickly and without breakdowns. Be realistic when assessing your needs, but if in doubt, go big.

Other than larger backhoe or large bucket lift implements, most of these tools are easily mounted on a tractor in a matter of minutes without wrenches, bolts, belts, or other encumbrances. Most are surprisingly inexpensive new, but check with your nearest farm store or tractor dealer. Good, used stuff is frequently available, and these salesmen are used to dickering over price. For example, recent prices for three-point tractor implements included a landscape rake for $350, a post hole digger for $360, and a 13,000-watt generator for $1,000.

Small-acreage tractors with all required features sell for anywhere from $8,000 to $20,000. Imported Korean, Chinese, or Russian tractors come in near the bottom of this price spectrum. These tend to be rough and ready but highly functional machines, frequently well worth the money under some circumstances. But don't consider purchasing any of these machines unless there is a dealer nearby. You want one that handles oil and fuel filters and on whose lot you can actually see the machines in operation.

There are some other important purchasing guidelines for potential tractor owners. As mentioned, be certain you are getting a standard three-point hookup system, standard power take-off capacity, and hydraulic lift system, and always purchase one with four-wheel drive. Most dealers don't even carry smaller two-wheel-drive models. If they have them, don't even look, price and shiny paint job notwithstanding. Four-wheel machines use their power more efficiently, are far more stable, and they don't tear up roads and lawns like two-wheel-drive machines.

You'll want a diesel engine. Diesels are cheaper to run and maintain than gasoline-powered machines, service on them is minimal, and they squeeze more work out of smaller engines. Fuel consumption for work produced is minimal compared to gasoline. Some owners refuel their diesel tractors only every month or two!

Use of diesel fuel does present a series of problems with which neophytes may be unaccustomed to dealing. Way back during my days on the farm, we made the mistake of accidentally dumping diesel fuel from 5-gallon cans into our gasoline-driven tractors. Didn't work well at all, and sure got Dad upset!

Dirt or water in the fuel is the biggest single problem for owners of small diesel tractors. Minute quantities of either can really raise hob. The remedy is to keep transport cans squeaky clean, use clean funnels, filter all fuel poured into the tractor, and replace the tractor's fuel filters as needed.

Red-colored diesel fuel is approved for off-the-road tractors. Basically clear fuel, perhaps with a greenish tint, is saddled with road taxes. Almost a dollar-per-gallon tax can be avoided if a source of red fuel can be found. I get mine from my replenished home-heating oil tank rather than from a pump in town. Tractor owners who anticipate the need can similarly purchase a used, 275-gallon, steel heating oil tank and have their bulk petroleum dealer fill it on a regular schedule. Even if you only have a couple of squeaky-clean 55-gallon barrels for diesel storage, build a 2 x 4 rack so they can be placed out of sight and still be used to gravity feed fuel directly into a tractor tank.

If you end up driving a diesel tractor to town to refuel, be aware that some filler nozzles at gas stations might be too large for your tractor's intake pipe. These high-volume pumps are designed to refuel 150-gallon truck tanks and will quickly overwhelm your small tractor's tank!

Tractor deployment in muddy, snowy, or otherwise slick conditions is best done with a set of rear tire chains. Purchase them from your local farm store or farm implement dealer. Expect to pay anywhere from $100 to $500 per pair, depending on size and make. I install mine loosely, then tighten them up with a bazillion rubber snubbers.

Dealers and tire people will attempt to persuade you otherwise, but I really like to have my tractor tires—both front and rear—filled with a calcium chloride solution. Tractor tires thus filled weigh twice as much or more than empty ones. As a result, traction and stability are improved dramatically. It costs from $15 to $40 each for solution and labor. On the other hand, calcium chloride-filled tires can be a real pain in the neck. The stuff is extremely corrosive to some materials, resulting in valve stems that must be replaced every four or five years before they start to leak. Weigh the pros and cons and make your own decision here.

Any punctured or flat tire is best handled professionally. Fortunately, tire people in farm country make house calls, even to small rural estates. If this isn't an option in your area, purchase a small flatbed trailer on which to haul your tractor to service people. Be sure the trailer frame and tires are more than adequate for the load.

Some tractor owners hire out their rigs and tools to neighbors for specific jobs. Services can include grading lanes, clearing snow, plowing or rototilling large gardens, spreading gravel, and spraying orchards. A couple of old men living near my home make a nice retirement income with their tractors. Performing these services requires a transport trailer.

Tractor maintenance is not difficult, but it can become an issue if several basic, inexpensive needs are neglected. Oil and filter must be changed every 60 to 80 hours of operation, and you can't take the machine to the 15-minute lube shop! Owners need to stock appropriate oil and filters and learn how to install both.

A grease gun and cartridges are also essential. Grease the appropriate lube points every month or so, depending on severity of service. Implements must also be greased on a regular schedule. Neglect greasing and you face expensive, time-consuming, inconvenient repairs. Cross bearings on power take-off shafts, for example, are frequently neglected, even though it takes less than 10 seconds to grease them.

These and other routine maintenance tasks (such as cleaning the engine sediment bulb thoroughly) may sound intimidating at first, but you'll be handling them in no time with some initial guidance from the tractor dealer or an experienced neighbor. Some repairs will require expert help, but if you stick to a scheduled cleaning and maintenance regimen, you should have few major problems. During the last 20 years, my only serious service need involved one tractor's electrical system. Worn sets of tires had to be replaced, but I consider that routine.

A final word about safety. Safety is always an issue, especially for folks with limited tractor operating experience. If you are diligent and careful while driving your machine, you will put yourself in no more danger than when operating any large work vehicle. That said, tractors can be purchased or fitted with rollover protection (i.e., roll bars) and seatbelts. At the very least, get a safety shield for the power take-off shaft. These powerful, rotating devices have ripped off arms and killed unfortunate folks who got their sleeves entangled in them. A PTO shield will prevent these accidents.

New tractor owners frequently discover to their surprise that operating a clean, well-maintained, modern tractor is interesting, rewarding, and fun. It is a good way to enjoy fresh country air (provided they are not doing something dusty and dirty like mulching brush on a dry August day) and get an astonishing amount of otherwise backbreaking work accomplished.

Chapter Twelve

Tools and Labor

Rural people tend to be tool junkies. Fantasizing about individual items listed in a good, thick tool catalog is a favorite indoor occupation. Signing up for these catalogs is not even necessary. Most of us with a rural address receive at least one fat tool catalog in the mail every few weeks.

Bragging is not the issue when neighbors spend a great deal of their social time demonstrating their most recent tool purchases. Rural folks intuitively realize that valuable information is there for the taking. All they need to do is keep their mouths shut and observe. Newcomers to the country embarking on their first betterment or maintenance project may not find this pastime to be as boring and provincial as they might at first suppose.

Borrowing tools, along with expert advice about how best to proceed on a project, is common out in the country. Giving and getting advice is relatively simple—all rural folks I know are willing to help if they can. However, tool borrowing is a complex issue.

Generally, you won't get to borrow tools when you are perceived as being so green and inexperienced that you would be a menace to yourself and to the tools, or when you don't have tools to loan in return. Those who comfortably integrate themselves into the community have a much easier time at it. Give it a few years after moving in. All of this seems to sort itself out nicely over time.

To borrow or buy a certain tool is usually dictated by the nature and scope of the task at hand. A guy with 1,200 fence posts to set will probably want to purchase his own tractor-mounted post hole auger. The fellow with three or four posts to place is best off borrowing or renting. Same is true of the property owner with half a cord of wood to split versus the fellow with 10 cords annually. That large-volume guy had better get his own wood splitter—either that or get turned down the next time he asks a neighbor to use his.

If you do borrow a tool from somebody, there are specific rules of etiquette and common courtesy that always apply. Return the tool promptly and in better condition than when you borrowed it (as in clean, sharpened, with a full tank of gas, fresh oil—whatever applies to the tool at hand). If you break the took, you bring back a new one. Don't ask first, because someone who was gracious enough to loan it probably won't ask you to replace it. Just bring a new one. Remember that the person from whom you borrowed the tool may use it to earn his living, so following these simple rules will not go unappreciated.

Some people collect tools the way others collect stamps or antiques. Every rural and perhaps some urban communities have their tool collectors. These are the guys with dozens and dozens of modern, basically unused hand and power tools in their basements or garages. One fellow near here even has a collection of tractor-mounted tools. Many have never been used even once; he just likes to know he can do a job quickly when necessary. He also likes to study mechanical devices, and—truth to say—there is pride of ownership. Tractor tools rather than a Corvette and all of that. Neighbors who get to know the fellow report he is easy to borrow from, almost as if he is anxious to finally find a purpose for the tool and justify its purchase.

Knowing how to use tools and how to organize a project so that it is completed in the best, cheapest, most efficient manner is very important. When we were growing up on the farm, we had a saying: "You need a carpenter, mechanic, electrician, plumber, or cabinetmaker? Just look in the mirror!" At least two changes have occurred since those times that have altered things dramatically.

First, all of those trades have become dramatically more technical and complex. Unsupervised, on-the-job training doesn't work like it used to when you factor in things like computerized diagnostics and modern tools that are more job-specific, better designed, and more powerful than their earlier counterparts.

Second, all of us have a great deal more money with which to hire outside help. These experts bring with them the right specialty tools and, more importantly, supplies and materials that, when installed, will last far longer in far harder service than anything we had in the past. Securing advice from neighbors and watching professionals in action are ideal methods of learning, but don't be surprised if even that is not enough training to do the job properly yourself next time.

Dad used to say that average farmers would have quickly worked themselves to death had their tools and equipment not broken down so frequently. Breakdowns and resulting work stoppages gave farmers the only rest they ever got. These days, properly functioning tools and gear can and do last for decades. Farmers and rural residents no longer have to endure frequent serious breakdowns.

Yet it is also a rule that tools and equipment take a greater beating out in the country. As a practical matter, the days of purchasing cheaper, minimal quality tools suitable for suburban woes are over. You're going to need bigger, more powerful electric saws, power drills, sanders, grinders, weed eaters, power rakes, lawnmowers, and tow chains. Even such mundane tools as pipe wrenches and channel locks often die a more premature death out in the country. "Buy quality, buy once" is the advice from the heartland. Saves time running to town repeatedly, if nothing else.

Adequate, rugged tools for the job are only half the issue. The other half is developing a mentality that figures out how to get the job done in half the time with one fourth the effort in a manner that provides twice the quality and durability. Some rural folks believe these skills can never be learned, especially by older newcomers who have never lived in the country, yet I have seen many, many rural transplants who had already learned to putter and repair in their city homes who do very well out in the country. Figuring out all of this "stuff" becomes an enjoyable, challenging pastime for these people.

Goes without saying that all of us cannot be good electricians, plumbers, mechanics, foresters, cabinetmakers, welders, or whatever, as was common on the farm 60 years ago. Yet we will have to do some of these chores ourselves. All rural residents face times when emergency repairs must be completed and professional help is not available.

First, a good reference library stocked with how-to guidebooks is a must. Reader's Digest publishes excellent, comprehensive do-it-yourself and fix-it-yourself manuals that cover dozens of typical home projects and appliance repair and maintenance jobs. Time-Life puts out a more detailed home repair and improvement series of books on everything from plumbing and wiring to weatherproofing and advanced woodworking. Familiar outfits like Black & Decker and Better Homes and Gardens publish similar guides. With patience and the rights tools, and perhaps supplemented with any tips you can find on the Internet for your specific task, there is virtually no job you can't handle on your own. You say you're hopeless when it comes to this type of work? Fortunately, labor trading is still common in rural America. As one becomes familiar in the community, trading skills with neighbors becomes more likely. Most common skills are usually available in even tiny, remote rural areas. You might not have similar mechanical aptitude to trade in kind, but there's always things like house watching, baby or pet sitting, assisting with low-skill manual labor, and dozens of other chores where your assistance would be beneficial and appreciated.

Rural neophytes need to realize that they must put time, effort, and money into figuring out how to accomplish needed projects. Identifying ideal tools for the job is a major part of the challenge. Otherwise you might find yourself caught in a difficult project that turns into real drudgery. Few of us, myself included, would enjoy country life under such conditions!

Rural Vehicles

This chapter is about choosing and using a safe, practical vehicle in a rural context. I won't get bogged down in evaluating specific makes and models of four-wheel-drive (4WD) or sport utility vehicles (SUVs). Rather, I'll just discuss the various considerations that go into selecting one (or more) that's suitable for your new environment.

Unfortunately, a purely practical, multipurpose rural vehicle may no longer exist in the United States. Consider this recent episode. A friend of mine who writes for the 4WD/SUV trade recently attended an industry conference of journalists and automotive engineers. When the question was raised, "How many of you have a sport utility vehicle or light four-wheel-drive truck," most, if not all, of those present raised their hands. The answer to the next question, however, completely flummoxed my friend. Out of more than 400 participants, only nine people indicated "yes" when asked if they had *ever* had their 4WD vehicles off the road! Please note emphasis on the word *ever*!

Little wonder we can no longer find a multiple-purpose rural vehicle. Detroit and Japan seem intent on producing for the far larger pool of city and suburban owners who drive SUVs for prestige and show.

In our patch of the woods, we have our vehicle in 4WD every time we come home from town, and we take it off the road at least once a week. Four-wheel isn't essential all times of the year, but negotiating unavoidable ruts and holes, powering through gripping mud, and traveling in slick winter conditions is safe and certain in 4WD.

Not all rural residents will require 4WD capability. Some people will move to relatively flat, open country serviced by well-maintained, hard-surfaced roads. Might be that they live south of the nation's snow belt and not even have to worry about ice or snow drifts. And it's a fact that some country drivers get along just fine with their two-wheel-drive autos equipped with ordinary tires and perhaps tire chains on really bad days. But having 4WD at one's disposal on the really awful weather days or under the worst road conditions provides great confidence that vehicle and driver will get to town and back safely and reliably.

In most instances there will be far more work for the family bus than just transportation. So much of this work will be of such a specific nature that some rural people end up with two or three machines. You might, for instance, want to mount a snowplow, brush guard, or winch on your vehicle. These roles are better served by a working "beater" vehicle rather than the family get-to-town rig. That way you don't have to continually mount and dismount the plow or other accessory, and the requisite dings and dents that come with such labor are of no concern to anyone.

Perhaps you don't anticipate such hard-use needs. Yet consider some of the home projects you might undertake that will require hauling gravel, firewood, lumber or other building materials, plants and shrubberies, mulch, animal feed, or whatever. Some people will want to pull a flatbed trailer loaded with snowmobiles, ATVs, or the tractor. There is also the boat, camper, or horse trailer to tow, and dozens of similar chores for the typical country vehicle. Take an experienced hand's advice: there will be lots of stuff to haul and many loads to pull. You will need a wagon that's up to the job.

After years of driving all sorts of vehicles, all of ours are now heavy 4WDs. Reliability is the key. The added certainty that we won't be sidetracked, waste time, or be deterred is important. We want to be as certain as possible that we can handle any project or overcome tough, unforeseen difficulties, and that we can do so efficiently and safely.

Standard cars or light SUVs that urban transplants may already own are temporarily okay after a move to the country. If nothing else, they buy time for rural neophytes to figure out exactly which duties and chores their vehicle should perform. Yet my guess is that after a few exasperating sessions high centered in snow or on rocks, all the family drivers will insist on more clearance, protective rock guards under the engine, better and larger tires, more horsepower, and maybe even high-capacity alternators, a limited-slip differential, and a winch!

Also bear in mind that rural vehicles wear out much faster than those driven only on hard-surfaced roads in town. General maintenance will be more extensive and expensive. Body bolts need to be retightened after driving washboarded, potholed roads. Shock absorbers, universal joints, air cleaners, and fan belts all wear faster. You will be dealing with glass repair services for windshield chips and cracks from driving on gravel roads much more frequently.

Here's another issue you might not have considered. My daughter was once briefly enamored with a career Marine who had no experience living in the country. Like many young military men, he treasured his wheels, making every effort to keep them spotless and shiny. Their relationship ruptured in part because he found that every time he drove our rural gravel lane, he had to spend hours washing, vacuuming, and detailing his car. After he left, a neighbor remarked that the fellow went back to the city where cars are clean and the air is dirty! If keeping your vehicle spotless is a compulsion—or even a priority—living at the end of a dusty, sometimes muddy, sloppy lane may not be for you.

Tough-use jobs and atrocious road conditions won't be the only things that take a toll on your vehicle. People living in the sticks simply put a great many more miles on their rigs than city people. It may, for instance, take a 20-mile round trip to get groceries, go to a high school football game, visit the doctor, or have the car serviced. If you have to drive younger kids to school, it becomes a daily issue. A city guy from Richmond, Virginia, recently remarked that we rural folks had to be careful about our driving. "Only place I know where it takes a quarter tank of gas to go get gas," he observed.

With all this driving long distances and bumping up and down dusty country roads, your tires are going to take a serious beating. Standard two-ply highway tires fail to hack it on crummy back-country roads and wear quickly. One set on a new Dodge truck lasted us only 3,000 miles! Rural drivers generally favor heavy six- and eight-ply off-road mud and snow tires. These beasts can handle most any conditions, but they do have their downsides: they are expensive to purchase, they are noisy on the highway, and they can produce an uncomfortable ride.

There have been a few times in 40 years when heavy snow prevented me from being able to make it home even with 4WD and sturdy tires. At times I parked at the neighbors' and walked. One time I sucked it up and purchased a new set of tire chains in spite of the fact that a near new set already hung in the barn at home. Now I always carry tire chains through the snow season. A separate set of studded snow tires used exclusively for the winter might also fill the bill. If you go with chains, I recommend practicing putting them on in good weather in your driveway. You don't want your first experience with them to be at night in a sleet storm, with cold hands fumbling and passing cars splashing slush on you.

What are some other features to consider for your country rig? Pulling capacity is important, and this means having a sturdy hitch. You will need to pull someone else—or be pulled yourself—out of a snowbank or mud hole on occasion. In that regard, I am amazed that some rural folks still try to make do with wimpy bumper hitches rather than stout ones that bolt to the frame. Use a bumper hitch and risk having the entire bumper yanked out of shape, perhaps clipping a side panel as it goes, when you're pulling or being pulled.

Which type of transmission to choose is a heated topic for many people. I maintain that automatic trannies allow manufacturers to install wimpy, weak engines. Automatics prevent drivers from making specific adjustments to difficult driving conditions. Fuel economy is better with manual transmissions, and they cost less than automatics. Of the few automatic transmission vehicles I have owned, most have broken down in tough service. Other than the sixth-handed 1947 Universal Jeep I once owned, no manual rig of mine has ever lost its transmission.

America's driving public is firmly on the other side of this issue. Few Americans choose manual transmissions these days—so few that almost all models of automobiles and SUVs come only with automatic trannies. Personally, I feel betrayed and neglected by an auto industry that offers only automatics. I would, for instance, own a Jeep Grand Cherokee in a heartbeat if one were offered with stick shift.

In conclusion, anticipate that rural living will require a different, more capable personal vehicle than what you're accustomed to driving. Understand that a great many more difficult chores will be asked of the vehicle under much more adverse circumstances, and remember that you may find yourself stuck in tough circumstances with little help beyond your own abilities. (It's important to note that motor club rescuers like AAA take longer to respond to distress calls from rural areas.) With these facts as givens, nothing provides a greater sense of security than having the correct and adequate vehicle for the job.

Having said all this, it is still virtually impossible to predict exactly which vehicle will ideally suit your specific circumstances. Sometimes the hauling capacity of a truck will be needed. Other times a truck will be overly big and lack maneuverability. In an ideal world, a total of three vehicles will cover all the bases: a reliable 4WD SUV for everyday driving, a 4WD truck for heavy labor, and a rugged, purpose-designed rig such as a Jeep Universal for off-road travel. Most folks can't afford this many vehicles. In times past, many of the beneficial attributes of all these vehicles could be found in one machine. I am still looking for that vehicle.

Chapter Fourteen

Driving Protocol in the Country

Because people in the country spend so much of their time driving long distances, a rural road protocol of sorts has evolved. Unwritten rules apply that rural drivers follow rigorously—sometimes overtly, sometimes subconsciously. Unless you wish to be thought of as crude, rude, and socially unacceptable, you, the newcomer, must also learn and follow these rules.

First, absolutely do not roar up and down the road, no matter how important or hurried you deem yourself to be. Drive only as fast as the average neighbor. The only exceptions are emergencies like ferrying a sick kid to the hospital. Fast driving wreaks havoc on the condition of gravel and dirt lanes, and there's always the possibility of suddenly coming upon livestock, wildlife, or slow-moving farm equipment in the road. So slow down.

Absolutely without fail, smile and wave at every other driver you encounter on small country roads. This might seem odd for some women, but you will be perceived as warm and friendly, not promiscuous and forward. Smiling and waving may be the only contact you have for years at a time with some neighbors. The wave need not be much—just drape a hand over the top of the steering wheel and raise it as you approach the other car. Forget this waving and smiling business once on the main road.

Most of the time, rural people drive down the center of gravel roads, especially when slick, wintry conditions prevail. When driving rural roads in the middle, look far into the distance, alert for any oncoming traffic. On blind hills or curves, start a slow, gentle swing to the right until your sight distance improves, then gently swing back to the middle. Make way for oncoming traffic or anyone who wants to pass as needed.

Driving in the middle really is a safe system, developed over years of country driving. It prevents being spun off the road by snow or loose gravel, as it does against falling into a roadside ditch that looks safe because the plow left a level snow floor over the hole. Momentary loss of control on slick roads is more easily accommodated when you are driving safely out in the middle of the road, leaving you more margin for correction on both sides.

Whenever someone is walking along a country road, stop and ask if they would like a ride. I realize this is extremely difficult for many city people, but remember that rural people tend to get enough exercise without additional walking or jogging. Walkers are probably in distress, in which case it's your duty to help.

Similarly, rural drivers absolutely must stop and try to assist stuck or stranded motorists. Newcomers cannot afford the social risk of not helping. It's an absolute law of proper rural behavior. Even women must stop and offer what assistance they can. No compromise here if you genuinely want to be an accepted part of the neighborhood.

Granted I am from an older school of thinking on this matter and perhaps adhere to halcyon standards of my youth. One must exercise common sense and caution in this day and age. If the wanderer or stuck motorist looks shady and is not a familiar member of the community, or perhaps you recognize him as the fellow who's in and out of the hoosegaw on methamphetamine charges, better to pass on by. You can always call the non-emergency police number from your cell phone and report a possible motorist in distress if you don't feel comfortable stopping yourself.

This issue raises another rural caution. You never know when it will be *your* vehicle that breaks down, gets stuck, hits a deer, or has a flat. Your cell phone might not have service in remote areas, so always be prepared to walk. Even in nice weather, carry along a good pair of walking shoes and warm sweater or jacket, gloves, and other inclement-weather gear in your vehicle. A flashlight with spare batteries, water, and a bit of food are also handy. If weather or other circumstances necessitate that you wait it out in your car, these items (plus perhaps a blanket or two) will make you more comfortable until help arrives.

How, you may ask, does this relate to proper road protocol? Because it makes you *self-sufficient,* a handy trait (not to mention reputation) to have in the countryside. This way, too, if someone comes upon you walking down the road or sitting in your vehicle, all they'll have to do is give you a ride or get you unstuck. No rushing you to the hospital with hypothermia, inconveniencing and possibly endangering themselves in the process.

On the subject of rescues, rural road protocol includes carrying along tow straps, rugged 12,000- to 18,000-lb. test cloth bands used to pull vehicles. Because they are somewhat elastic, they are dramatically easier and less destructive to use than chains or cables. Tow straps are also ridiculously inexpensive and space efficient. It costs less than $20 each for heavy duty ones at car parts discounters or Wal-Mart. If you come across a stuck car, you'll have the right tools to assist with a rescue.

If somebody spends a significant amount of time pulling *you* out of a snowy ditch or mending crusty, battered connections on your dead battery, it's proper, if only for form's sake, to offer them a little something for their troubles. A small amount of cash (no more than $5 or $10) so they can buy themselves coffee or a cold beer should do it. Nine times out of ten they will appreciate the offer but refuse it. (The tenth person will really need the cash.) They'll probably just remind you to help somebody else in distress someday. If the assist requires they provide you with a part more substantial than a spare bolt or some twists of wire, get their address and make arrangements to replace the item as soon as you get home.

Country newcomers will be amazed by the number of miles and hours they will spend behind the wheel of their car or truck. It's a price most of us are happy to pay for the peace and solitude of rural life. Following the local customs of the road will help you fit into your new community that much easier. These protocols may seem strange, but social ramifications abound if they are not adhered to.

Chapter Fifteen

Resupply

Going to town to purchase parts and supplies can be a real pain, especially from very remote locations. As a result, country people develop a batch of tricks to minimize this sort of running around.

One not-so-secret trick is to shop by mail. We have all heard about the old Sears catalog and its vital role in comfortable country life. Rural folks know that local stores frequently do not carry many items in the numbers, sizes, and colors they require. There is no Home Depot across town with 20 varieties of electrical outlet boxes, wood stain, or whatever widget it is you require. Major items like window or door casings can get expensive if you only have one remote supplier to choose from. This fact of country life is often a shock to newcomers.

Sears's big book is history, but rural residents still collect catalogs of all kinds from which they can order vital goods, and they've learned to use the Internet and UPS like the rest of the civilized world. Nowadays these catalogs and Web sites tend to be ones selling hardware, tools, tractor parts, and supplies unique to a specific family need, such as home canning or gunsmithing. We like to shop this way for computer and camera supplies, seeds, crop additives, and office supplies.

All of this neglects the core issue facing rural newcomers: that is, recognizing that they cannot beat themselves and their vehicles to pieces by frequently running to town to merchants who likely don't have needed items anyway. Shopping from catalogs does not alleviate our need for prior planning. If anything, it confirms it.

True enough, overnight delivery is available virtually everywhere. As compared to even 20 years ago, overnight mail service greatly simplifies rural life. But at what cost? At times, the added expense for overnight delivery can be easily justified. But like other aspects of country life, use this plan too often and be in danger of exceeding a limited budget.

The real trick is to identify who can supply your specific needs in the shortest possible time at the best price, then set up a plan to funnel supplies into your household without fuss or undue hardship. Like so many of life's issues, establishing a home resupply system is easy to describe but difficult to implement. Yet let's assume you are a reasonably organized person, highly motivated to make your country sojourn as pleasant as your dreams. Here is how seasoned country people go about keeping themselves stocked in food, spare parts, and other essentials.

Insofar as possible, attempt to anticipate routine trips to town and combine them with such chores as picking things up, ordering needed items for pickup later, or securing repairs. Many people work in town. While there, there's no reason not to drop off the dry cleaning and order or pick up insulation, new mower blades, or whatever on your way to and from the job. Same for the soccer mom taking kids to practice every Monday, Wednesday, and Friday. Make it a habit to look at the chore list or to ask everyone what they need. Nothing terribly profound about this, except some city slickers seem unused to this level of coordination and cooperation.

Next, start writing down what you and your family typically need to stock up on each week. Even a weekly plan is tough for many folks used to popping in to their local supermarket or hardware store on a moment's notice for tonight's dinner makin' or a pound of sixpenny nails, but it's where you need to begin. This list will encompass your common consumables like groceries and liquor and things like gas for the car. From there, you can extend it out to important but less-used items. How much flour, sugar, salt, baking powder, cooking oil, matches, vitamins, toothpaste, soap, freezer paper, razors, bug spray, mothballs, Scotch tape, deodorant, etc., do you use in a week, month, or six months? What about prescription or over-the-counter medicines? Figure it out and write it down.

Some folks, ourselves included, try to double buy whenever we see a good deal in the supermarket on something we think should go in our supply larder. It's a sound concept, but it leads us to having 11 cans of Bar Keepers Friend powdered cleanser and 14 big cans of pie cherries on the shelf—an eight years' supply at present rates of consumption! Try to restrain yourself better than we do.

Rural residents require a great deal more home storage space than their city cousins. It goes with the territory. Many existing country homes already have spacious, old-fashioned pantries. There might also be an additional storage area in the basement, garage, or utility shed.

Do not allow your limited storage space to fill with items that are not rotated through regularly. At times this rotation is infrequent, but 14 cans of pie cherries or 11 cans of cleanser is inexcusable.

Storage space will also be needed for collections of excess nuts and bolts, drive belts, spare blades, wire, solder, and a million similar shop-type items. It can be expensive, exasperating, and time consuming to have to run to town every time a piece of equipment requires relatively minor service or repair. Have the stuff on hand and save yourself time, money, and grief.

I stock two years' worth of oil, filters, grease, and spare parts for the tractor because we have spent years thinking in terms of anticipating our needs. Yet unanticipated snafus are also a part of living far from town, as a recent experience repairing our tractor-mounted lawn mower shows.

After 14 years of service, a bearing on the rotating cutter drum wore out. Removing the old bearing without a unique tool proved impossible. It was off to town for the tool and, of course, a new bearing. Might as well make as few trips as possible.

When I got home, I discovered it was the wrong tool. I couldn't get upset since the shop loaned me the tool at no cost. Purchased new it cost close to $100, and delivery would have taken six days.

Back to town a second time, on a day when there was plenty to do without scaring up bearing pullers. This time the bearing removed with little effort or problem . . . but the new replacement was wrong. Not seriously wrong, but enough wrong that I couldn't use it. Back to town a third time for the correct bearing. Four hours later, the mower was repaired and ready to go.

I inventory critical parts and supplies as religiously as anyone, but there is no practical way to anticipate the sudden need for a single bearing or an expensive tool used once every 14 years! Sometimes we rural dwellers just have to suck it up and do three trips to town in a morning.

How do *really* remote rural folks make do? I'm talking about elderly, reclusive, or deep-woods people who get to town every six months on average. Besides keeping careful, detailed consumption rate records for both the house and shop and stocking a huge number of items (their shelves groan with extra alternators, buckets of detergent, light bulbs, antifreeze, gloves, toothpaste, canned milk, and so on), these people become expert at identifying and keeping track of people who regularly travel to resupply areas. As such, truck drivers, rangers, pilots, boat operators, and similar types routinely haul supplies back for them. They are not afraid to ask for help since they do likewise when they are going in that direction, asking around before going to town themselves to determine who needs what.

Established rural residents living only a few miles from town frequently deploy a variation of this plan. Folks who have kids in a number of different after-school activities are often the instigators. In our area, kindergarten moms got the program up and running.

Informal carpools develop wherein a parent with the least pressing schedule picks up all the kids on the road. While in town, they may be asked to pick up a roll of brown wrapping paper, a box of diapers, or 5 pounds of sixpenny nails for another parent. It is done without fuss or muss.

I fully understand that this level of informal cooperation might be incomprehensible to folks newly arrived from the city. You may not even know a sixpenny nail if one dropped on your toe. But watch for it. It really happens. And you can and will do it, too.

A final word about storage before we move on. Detailed guidelines for the proper storage of food and supplies are far beyond the scope of this book. There are many books and Web sites dedicated solely to the topic. I will only touch upon some very basic issues just to give you an idea of what it entails. For more information, read books like *Food Storage 101* or visit the food storage FAQ at Web sites like www.survival-center.com. Similar resources are available for nonconsumable items.

Depending on the climate and the quality of storage facilities at your rural paradise, deterioration of shelf goods may be an issue. Climate control is imperative. Without it, stored food can deteriorate, sometimes in an incredibly short period of time. Hot temperatures can adversely affect canned goods, and cans will rust in humid areas, allowing spoilage agents to enter and ruin the food within. Canned food will spoil up north if left to freeze. No matter where you are, six months' worth of flour, sugar, dried beans, peas, or lentils may be invaded by bugs or mice unless they are stored properly. Dog food left in original paper bags will attract mice, rats, and ground squirrels. And it's not just food: in wet climates, precision metal parts will rust and corrode due to the incessant moisture.

What's the secret to safe storage? Again, it's too big a topic to cover completely here, but many people routinely store bulk commodities or delicate electrical or steel parts in heavy, tightly sealed plastic or metal cans. For food, the container has to be "food grade," meaning it will not transfer nonfood chemicals into the food and contains no hazardous chemicals or residues. For large quantities, I suggest 20- to 30-gallon heavy plastic garbage containers with good, solid lids. You'll find these at Wal-Mart, Target, and similar outlets.

Some items should not be stored together. Apples and potatoes are a classic example. Apples contain a natural chemical that breaks dormancy in potatoes. It causes them to sprout early with greater enthusiasm, deteriorating the spuds as a source of food.

Obviously, do not store cans of fuel near firewood. It is dangerous, of course, to store the combustible fuel next to the wood, but dust and debris from the wood can also contaminate the fuel.

Many rural residents own one or more large freezers. Freezing is a quick, easy, safe way to preserve garden vegetables, meat from that cow you raised and had butchered, extra venison from the deer hunter down the road, or frozen supplies hauled from town. Folks new to the country don't seem to anticipate the need for a large freezer, but those who stick it out often end up with two or even three large ones.

Rural veterans develop great skill at accommodating these supply issues. They get very good at knowing when and where to purchase vital items, as well as how to store them properly and safely. Newcomers should learn from them and adopt this simple but important way of doing things.

Chapter Sixteen

Critters

Critter control is often the single most overlooked and difficult problem for newcomers to the country. Rural homeowners
who take too long to deal with pesky creatures may find their
yards destroyed by moles, ground squirrels, deer, or—my least
favorite—a flock of greedy, noisy, dirty, green-poop-emitting
Canada geese that have permanently moved in.

Let's start with two of the most common critters you are likely to encounter in your new surroundings: mice and rats. Put simply, rats and mice cannot be left to multiply in close proximity to
humans. The potential for damage and disease is too great.

There are two distinct kinds of mice in the United States. Most
folks are familiar with common gray house mice. These are the
relatively ugly, obnoxious little critters that initially came to North
America with early settlers from Europe. Every state and province
in North America has populations of house mice.

Deer mice are their distant cousins. These are cute, sloe-eyed
little critters, reddish brown to chocolate colored, with white
underbellies. They do not have the long, scaly tails characteristic
of house mice that most people find so objectionable. There are
scores of subspecies of deer mice, which is of interest to only a
handful of scientists who study rodents.

The problems these little guys can cause cannot be understat-
ed. Both domestic and deer mice spoil a great deal by raiding and
fouling food supplies. Each mouse produces thousands of fecal
pellets per year, and their little puddles of dried urine are everywhere. They chew house insulation and wiring, make noise at
night, create costly sanitary cleanup chores among the crockery,
and, worst of all, carry deadly hantavirus and Lyme disease. Lyme
disease is a bit different than hantavirus—transmission occurs courtesy of ticks carried by deer mice rather than by direct contact
with mouse droppings.

Mice eat virtually anything. They consume all kinds of grains,
fruit, vegetables, carrion, and most, if not all, man-made food items.
Pet food left lying around the house or cabin is a major attraction

and sometimes the principal source of nourishment for mice. Mice will even scarf up old or carelessly stored leather goods.

Noting chew evidence on unprotected food in the kitchen is generally the first clue there is a mouse problem. Next it's their copious urine and feces production. There may be tracks, hair, and chew damage to other parts of the house.

Although I genuinely like and admire most all wild creatures, it is tough for me to concede much benefit to rats. They are called Norway rats, brown rats, house rats, barn rats, sewer rats, gray rats, and wharf rats. The nesting, feeding, and breeding characteristics of the different species can be unique, but we will consider all under one heading as rats.

Like mice, rats eat virtually anything and everything. Not only do relatively large rats consume a great deal of valuable food-stuffs, they contaminate great quantities of food. Their incessant digging and chewing can cause structural damage to homes and other buildings.

Rural folks do not have to be wildlife biologists to recognize the signs that they have rats. There will be chew damage to wires, insulation, siding, and flooring. Tunneling and digging will damage floors and foundations. Food stores may be contaminated with rat droppings, copious half-inch, elongated, brown or black pellets.

There are three principal methods for dealing with mice and rats effectively. All three should be deployed simultaneously.

First and foremost, isolate all food from the critters. Absolutely everything rats and mice find edible must be placed in rodent-proof steel or heavy plastic containers. This includes pet food and garbage, two of their most frequently overlooked food sources. Don't forget things like garden seeds, decorative dried corn, and other dried fruits and vegetables. If it can't be placed in securely sealed, rodent-proof containers, construct a barrier fence around it with quarter-inch wire-mesh hardware cloth. Use the same hardware cloth along with some tin to barrier all holes in the foundation and walls of your home so that the critters have a tough time getting in.

The few rats and mice that struggle to gain access to your premises, only to find nothing there to eat, are controllable. Poison is cheaper, easier, and more effective than any other method for controlling occasional itinerant rats and mice. When, for one reason or another, poisons are unavailable or unacceptable, common snap traps or small cage-type live traps (such as the Havahart line) are fine. So long as you check and maintain the traps frequently, success will be yours. Captured critters can be transported to the woods and released alive if that better fits your philosophy.

Modern rat and mouse poison isn't as hazardous to handle and deploy as in times past. It is very effective in minute doses, nonthreatening to nontarget animals, and leaves little to no residue danger. Most important, today's baits are very, very palatable to both rats and mice.

Ramik (commonly called "green bait"), Assault, Maki, Contrac, RoZol, and Ditrac are the trade names of some of these products. Read the labels and look under active ingredients for materials such as brodifacoum, bromadiolone, chlorophacinone, or diphacinone. All are equally effective.

Making the emotional decision to deal with rats and mice is easier than making that same decision relative to many other wild critters you will likely encounter in the country.

Take deer, for instance. Having deer quietly graze on your front lawn may be a dream of yours, but prolific, uncontrolled, shrubbery-munching deer have become a serious problem in much of rural America. Not only do they devastate gardens, they pose a hazard to motorists and can occasionally become aggressive toward unknowing folks who approach too close. State Fish and Game people do not have the manpower, budget, or political muscle to deal with deer in rural subdivisions. In some newer residential areas in the country, culling problem deer through hunting has been banned, yet so-called "earth friendly" techniques such as feeding them birth control pills are expensive, ineffective, and cruel. (Young affected deer perish in the winter.)

All sorts of things have been tried to keep nuisance deer away from gardens and greenery. Wire fencing is the usual choice, around either the entire property or just the ravaged garden. Deer can clear astonishing heights when they jump, so the fence needs to be 10 to 15 feet high. If a high wire fence surrounding your yard sounds unsightly, individual shrubs and trees can be protected with wire barriers. You can also try commercial chemical repellents such as Hinder.

Geese can be a tricky matter because federal migratory game laws severely restrict your ability to do anything about them once they have decided to take up residence on your lawn or pond. You need to deal with the situation before it becomes a real problem by not allowing a pair of benign geese to become 50 to 100 or more noisy, pooping nuisances. People have resorted to noise-making cannons, humanlike scarecrows with flapping clothes and noise makers (pie plates, bells, etc.), and streaming strips of Mylar to ward flocks off to other areas. A dog allowed to run loose on the grounds can prevent geese from congregating, but be sure this tactic doesn't run you afoul of the game laws mentioned above.

For big predators, denying them access to their food source is the key. For bears, that means securing garbage, barbeque grills, pet food, hummingbird feeders, and other smelly attractions commonly left outdoors. For cougars, it means controlling the deer around your place and keeping your pets (and young children) closely monitored or completely indoors at dawn and dusk and into the evening, when these big cats are most active. If these food sources are made available on your land, hungry predators will follow them to your door eventually.

Of course there's much more to this topic. What about coons ruining the roof and chimney, squirrels that steal fruit and nuts from the orchard, skunks in the garage, prairie dogs tunneling under the driveway, and porcupines that kill trees in the orchard and fill the dog's mouth with quills? A neighbor really wanted to keep some showy peafowl, but resident hawks and owls kept eating the chicks. I could go on and on about abatement techniques for all sorts of critters, but I've made my point. Dealing with problem animals is as much a part of living in the country as enjoying their magnificent presence.

My personal decision is to attempt to live in harmony with the critters around us. When we must deal with them, we do so with gentleness and discretion. Like anyone else, we enjoy seeing deer, elk, bear, and owls, yet we take reasonable measures to prevent them from making us ill, destroying our property, or menacing our safety. Now that you are aware of the issue, you can do the same.

Chapter Seventeen

Crime and Security

So you've made the move from the congested, dirty, crime-infested city to a lush, green, peaceful country paradise! Yet before you can relax completely, you, the newcomer, have some nagging doubts concerning the validity of a couple of stereotypes about crime in the country, namely that rural residents don't lock their homes and vehicles or unduly concern themselves with security. After years of living a necessarily cautious life characteristic of the big city, leaving that baggage behind can be tough.

Well, like so many things about rural life, it isn't nearly that easy. It is true that many rural folks have a highly developed sense of property rights, practically precluding a criminal mentality and culture that preys on citizen neighbors. It is also true that a significant percentage of rural homes are protected by firearms and by residents willing to use them in their defense. Let's look at both of these issues in turn.

The saga of Lisa Jones offers an example that may no longer be typical, but it does provide a starting point.

Ms. Jones was a farm wife and local newspaper editor/reporter who still lived on a working farm. Among her peers she was highly regarded as an astute writer, observer, and commentator. Numerous awards and recognitions validated that assessment.

In the second-to-last paragraph of one of her popular columns, Ms. Jones casually mentioned that she intended to be gone on vacation for the next four weeks and that, in keeping with rural custom at the time, they would probably not bother locking their home. She didn't say as much, but in all likelihood keys for their trucks and cars parked about the property were probably left on the seats or tucked in the vehicles' sun visors.

Oh, what a storm of controversy—mostly among those new to her rural community. On her return, Ms. Jones was severely castigated by readers not only for letting the world know she would be gone but also for mentioning that they don't lock their home.

Her response (which I'm paraphrasing here) was pure rural wisdom. "Our home," she pointed out, "is extremely hard to find.

It is located down obscure rural roads and a long private lane. Casual thieves would have a difficult time finding the place. If they did, they would have to use a vehicle to access the farmstead; no creeping in unawares at night. Any intrusion would be quickly noticed by the neighbors.

"Our security involves all of the neighbors knowing all of the vehicles common to our neighborhood. Bus drivers, mail carriers, and road maintenance workers add to the pool of people watching our place while we are gone," she said.

Was there danger of loss from professional thieves? Probably not, Ms. Jones suggested. "We don't keep anything of value at home that could be carried off in anything but a large truck," she said. Nevertheless, as something of an act of contrition, she agreed that they would start locking their home when away for extended periods. It would be easier to prove loss for insurance purposes with evidence of forced entry, she finally conceded.

Although I personally lock up only when gone more than two days running, I question even this level of security in rural areas. Throwing a heavy deck chair through a patio door or window makes a racket, but if your nearest neighbor is 2 miles away, what difference does it make to the burglar? Only rural homes protected by an expensive electronic web of security have a chance to thwart break-ins completely, but even then, homes with elaborate burglar alarms are not totally secure. Takes too long for authorities to respond to an alarm out in the sticks. If you've had a few false alarms (a common occurrence with these systems), they might not respond at all.

Relatives on my father's side who lived in Chicago maintain that they never notified the local police to "look after the place" when they were gone on vacation. Perhaps these were apocryphal tales, but these folks felt that Chicago coppers were prone to cooperate with thieves.

This isn't a realistic possibility with rural sheriff departments. Tremendous local constraints generally keep resident law enforcement officers honest—at least when dealing with county citizens. First, there is always the local gossip mill. If a deputy were in cahoots with the resident cat burglar, it wouldn't take long for people to put two and two together. Second, rural sheriffs and their deputies interface heavily with citizens by helping with emergencies, serving papers, dealing with traffic near road work sites, and performing routine patrols around the community. Unless they are particularly cold-blooded, mercenary individuals, this level of social interaction precludes local cops from preying on their neighbors (many of whom might be friends and relatives anyway). Running for election every four years is the third reason rural sheriffs tend to be honorable. If they weren't, again the rural gossip mill would kick in to high gear and they would not be reelected.

Besides, the police are seldom the first line of defense against crime in the countryside. Like their city counterparts, rural police expend their time and energy commensurate with the severity of the crime, and budgets are always extremely thin. In other words, don't expect a full-scale investigation over a vandalized mailbox or a garbage-dumping incident. (A crime of a truly horrible nature will generate the proper mobilization, the competence of which depends entirely on the quality and experience of the force.) So notifying the sheriff that you will be gone is not a bad idea, it just isn't productive. Better to rely on folks you know who are already around.

It's basically untrue that even multigenerational rural people never lock their homes. Many now do in this day and age. New transplants from the city or suburbs will likely secure their homes, and that's fine, even though locking itself is not a particular deterrent for a determined thief. The bottom line is that rural security is relaxed, informal, and practical—but certainly not absent.

Is extensive firearms ownership among homeowners a deterrent to crime in the country? The short answer is "probably." Numerous studies and polls of convicted felons have shown that criminals dislike the notion of confronting a homeowner during a burglary, especially if they think that homeowner might do something crazy like shoot them in defense of person or property.

That said, should city people who have never owned a gun consider buying one after moving to the country? Absolutely, if you're comfortable with the notion, but unless you have had prior training or experience with firearms, moving slowly is advisable.

Take a basic shooting course with a certified instructor at a gun range, which will include the fundamentals of firearm safety, handling, and shooting. Once you are comfortable with guns, visit a gun shop and spend some time with a knowledgeable clerk selecting the type of firearm that best suits your needs, whether it be a handgun, rifle, or shotgun.

Note that many country dwellers look on firearms more as tools than as personal defense items. Without appropriate tools, country life is much more difficult. For example, rural residents often resort to firearms when overpopulating gophers dig and churn the lawn, rabbits eat the garden, wild dogs threaten the geese, or it becomes necessary to dust an errant moose or deer out of the rose bed with a shotgun loaded with nonlethal salt. For these circumstances, think about a shotgun for the dogs and moose and a .22 rifle for the smaller critters. In fact, unless one becomes interested in guns, these two firearms will handle 99 percent of all rural needs.

While we're on the topic, let's take a closer look at the role guns play in country life.

Statistics indicate that approximately 50 percent of American households have at least one gun owner, and a significant percentage of rural Americans in that category believe strongly in the Constitutional right to keep and bear arms. The fact is, guns and all that go with them—hunting, self-defense, self-sufficiency, responsibility—are an ingrained way of life in rural America. If you are an active donor to Handgun Control, Inc. or have some beef with the NRA, you might consider when or even if you want to engage in debate on the topic of guns if your goal is to integrate yourself in the local community.

Whether or not gun ownership rates are higher in the country than the city is subject to debate, but it is a fact that you are more likely to encounter firearms out in the open in the country than you are in the city. Citizens who own guns in the boondocks are often unconcerned about carrying rifles and shotguns out in plain sight in their cars or trucks, something you simply will not encounter in urban areas today. There are hunters in the fields, and I am surprised at the frequency with which I encounter rural folks who carry concealed handguns legally. A plumber heating specialist, private school headmaster, lawyer, judge, retired neurosurgeon, dentist, carpenter, roofer, university bureaucrat, and accountant come immediately to mind.

Even though I have never lived in a crime-ridden, inner city area, I strongly suspect that rural residents hear the sound of gunfire more frequently than even those who live in really bad urban locations where residents report rival gangs firing away with reckless abandon. Gunfire is prohibited in some rural areas by local restrictive covenants, yet country folk who do not live in formal developments often take advantage of their wide-open spaces to sight in or practice with their guns.

As an example, neighbors hereabouts make it a particular point to initiate newcomers with a bit of gunfire. By so doing, they let them know both the character and orientation of the neighborhood. So far, only one objector has remained. He is mostly ignored.

A friend from Colorado reports a similar clash that took place in a boutique community that sprung up relatively recently in the midst of what had traditionally been working farmland. One morning, a new homeowner was jarred from his morning reverie of coffee and NPR by a salvo of shotgun blasts. It turns out he had moved in next to a swath of land owned by a family that had lived in the area for generations and who used their fields as a base for duck and goose hunting. Outraged sputtering to town authorities and the media got the newcomer nowhere. The hunting family was on the right side of the law and, interestingly, public opinion. "Move to the country, live with country ways," seemed to be the prevailing attitude.

The lesson? If occasional bursts of gunfire are threatening or annoying to you, perhaps you should reconsider living in the country.

If ours were still a thinly populated, agricultural-based society, exploring and explaining rural philosophies on crime would be much simpler. As it is, the rise of thousands of newcomers living in what amounts to large-acreage, high-density rural subdivisions complicates the issue tremendously. These are folks who live in the country but sometimes retain many city values and attitudes.

The prevailing attitude on security will depend on the mix. If it's mostly old-line ag-rural, that's the culture that will predominate. If it's increasingly suburban, the old-time values will eventually be forced out.

Readers must filter my comments on crime in the country through the fact that they are based on my personal experience in specific places at specific times. I am told, for instance, that the scourge of methamphetamine has reached truly frightening proportions in what were once quite backwoods regions. This insidious drug might turn people who, a generation or two ago, would have been the local down-and-outers—poor, but honest, harmless members of the community—into a serious threat for petty crime and even random violence as the addiction worsens. And I am not so naïve to think that we in the country don't have to worry about serious crime. We have our share of young vandals, drunken gunplay, horrible domestic abuse, armed robbery, brawls, rape, and worse. It's just that if you take reasonable precautions about security of property and self, exercise common sense when interacting with strangers, and mind your own business, the likelihood of becoming the victim of crime in the country is less than in the city or suburbs. Nothing revolutionary about that observation.

Chapter Eighteen

Major Natural Hazards

Serious forest fires blackened millions of acres in the West. Some, like those north of Spokane, Washington, swept into posh, tree-covered rural developments, torching scores of beautiful homes.

After the fires were brought under control, an area fire chief invited perhaps 50 rural residents in his jurisdiction to a meeting. "Let's discuss rural fire prevention and abatement measures," he said, "as well as the realistic response you can expect from the department in the event of a major wildfire."

Things went reasonably when the chief focused his discussion on such practical stuff as keeping garden hoses handy, installing fireproof roofs, removing brush, duff, and lower tree limbs from an area 150 feet in diameter around home sites on tree-covered lots, and dozens of additional self-help measures rural landowners could implement before wildfires threatened their property. He went on to outline plans to pump water from handy rural ponds and the importance of solid, well-maintained access lanes for heavy emergency vehicles. But the gathered group became a bit restive when the talk turned to specific measures planned by fire abatement people after fires were reported in the area.

"Our plan is to telephone each one of you to tell you when to evacuate," the chief explained. He was serious as a heart attack. Those in attendance looked as if they were having one.

The prevailing attitude was: *why?* Most residents in attendance already realized that every area has its own natural hazards to contend with, and that wildfires—not floods and probably not windstorms or earthquakes—were the ones they faced. They also knew—and the chief confirmed—that, with limited equipment at its disposal, the fire department saw little hope of containing a serious forest fire running loose in the home-studded rural areas.

An attendee patiently tried explaining the locals' perspective to the fire chief.

"We are aware that people in cities are sometimes collectively able to better deal with their natural disasters," our spokesman said (this because of higher concentrations of emergency equipment and helping hands), "but what about those of us who plan ahead and acquire backup generators, large-capacity wells, water storage capacity, auxiliary pumps, and high-volume hoses, and who install ponds, cut brush, and fireproof our roofs and who intend to fight to save our homes?"

The chief was well aware of the tough, independent nature of the people in the hall and sensed he was in a box. "Well," he finally said, "I would hate to do it, but maybe I would have to call the sheriff to have them forcibly evacuated."

Hearing that, possibly two thirds of the attendees vowed never, under any circumstances, to call the local fire department in the event of a fire. As an aside, that chief found other employment before year's end.

As the man at the meeting pointed out, most successful rural people are self-reliant types accustomed to dealing with natural disasters without waiting for outside help. Rural neophytes not inculcated with this attitude soon flee back to the city, where safety in numbers and faith in quick and efficient government assistance seems to be the rule. (Discussing whether that may not be a valid, workable philosophy is beyond the scope of this chapter!)

Natural disasters can encompass all sorts of phenomena, including flooding, mud slides, tornadoes, hurricanes, blowing sand, earthquakes, winter storms, droughts, brittle cold snaps, and volcanoes. Every region on earth has at least one natural disaster potential.

Successful rural residents determine which natural hazards are likely to affect them, then honestly plan to deal with or at least mitigate the risks. Flooding, for instance, is common in many places, where pristine, beautiful valleys instantly revert to ugly, brown, muddy holes. Wise landowners in these regions realize the inherent danger and keep their homes, barns, and even fences up out of the flood plain. If you live anywhere on the vast plains of middle America, you obviously must prepare your family and property for such things as tornados, violent lightning storms, and hail. The list goes on.

Some natural hazards are difficult to predict. In 1989, 92-mile-per-hour winds came through our portion of Idaho, the first time in recorded history. Our house and barn roofs were okay because of my propensity to overbuild, but 11 giant old trees were shattered. Our mountain thundered with roaring chain saws for days till the mess was cleared.

Mud slides are another classic example of unanticipated natural calamities. They occur infrequently, usually when major fires remove stabilizing brush, trees, grass, and duff from steep slopes. Unusually heavy late winter or early spring rains saturate unprotected ground before new ground cover can establish. Then it becomes a terrible disaster. Hundreds of feet of mountainside, comprising hundreds of tons of mud, rock, soil, trees, and junk, slump down into the land below. Everything in its path is carried away. Nothing, much less houses and barns, can be replaced on the mountainside.

A good homeowners' insurance policy is about the only protection against this type of calamity—and many policies don't cover natural disasters. Some localities try to mitigate these problems with strict zoning and building regulations. The presence of such might alert neophytes to dangers ahead, but don't count on it. Many regulations have little to do with reality, frequently promulgated by current residents who already have their dream homes in the country and do not want others moving in near them.

If there is a question about natural hazards in the area you are considering and good answers do not seem to be forthcoming, go to several local insurance agents and talk about full coverage on all risks. What they will and won't cover may give you some hints of what lies ahead. That and good old common sense will enable you to understand and prepare for any natural disasters you may have to face.

Outlining specific guidelines for every type of weather-related disaster is beyond the scope of this book. Numerous books and Web sites are available on this topic. (On the Web, start with the Federal Emergency Management Agency, better known as FEMA, or the Red Cross.) The lesson here is that country transplants need to adopt the self-sufficient mind-set of established, successful rural residents. One must be respectful and prudent about nature's wrath, but that does not mean being intimidated or frightened by it.

A classic example of this attitude occurred in the late 1960s at a place called Moscow Mountain, located deep within northern Idaho. People living in rugged mountains expect some heavy snows, but this one was exceptionally heavy, more than 8 feet in places.

During the slow, laborious snow-clearing operation, some emergency crew workers suddenly recalled a dirt-poor elderly widow living alone in a three-room log cabin way up on the mountain, cut off without power, light, or phone. They wondered if she was still okay, so four especially strong, able members of the local Civil Air Patrol stepped forward and volunteered to cross-country ski the 11 miles to her place and check on her well-being. (Today they would probably call up a helicopter or try snowmobiles. Things were different 40 years ago.)

After hours of hard work, they made it in to the little snow-covered cabin on the side of the mountain. They hollered their hellos and then knocked on the door. "Ma'am, we are from the Red Cross," they explained.

"Oh, I am very sorry," she responded. "I see you have come a long, difficult way, but I just cannot give you a donation this year. But do step in for a cup of warm coffee!"

Such intrepidness among a broad segment of rural dwellers has roots stretching back centuries, but today's version has at least one foot in the survival movement of the '70s and '80s. This was a time when determined rural do-it-yourselfers closely evaluated their preparedness in the event of a nuclear war with the Soviet Union. Preparedness, in this instance, included a self-reliant mindset; a small library of informational volumes on everything from raising rabbits for food to alternate energy sources; stored food, water, clothing, and fuel supplies; and a definite plan for toughing it out in the new world of a nuclear wasteland.

Most rural residents today are not concerned about a nuclear holocaust, but they still must be prepared for the real problems that result from power outages due to storms and natural disasters. Alaskans, for example, need to keep their oil furnaces operating in winter and freezers in summer. Without electricity in the winter, their homes might freeze; if the freezer quits in summer, they lose their food. Residents of the dry, mountainous American West need uninterrupted access to electrical power so they can pump enough water to save their home in the face of wildfires that sometimes race through the region.

In both situations, rural residents have discovered that a small amount of self-generated electrical power will add to their safety and quality of life if and when a disaster strikes, and that means owning a generator. Maintaining safety and comfort under temporary disaster conditions involves providing for food, water, shelter, and warmth. Generators see to provision of food, water, and warmth. Unless it is a total wipeout situation, your home is the shelter.

Generator ownership is far from universal among rural residents, yet those who have been through a disaster or who may have a motor home or camper are many times more likely to own one. Just remember that fires, floods, earthquakes, ice storms, hurricanes, tornadoes, and other natural disasters have an insidious tendency to suck all emergency equipment out of the supply pipeline. During recent flooding in the Midwest, generators from as far away as southern California were cleaned off dealers' shelves. Retail stores reported calls asking if they had display models on the floor that could be shipped out to disaster areas.

We discussed generators in depth in Chapter 5. For now, the important point for country newcomers is to identify potential natural hazards in the area, evaluate the likelihood that they will suffer from them, then think about mitigation measures. Adapting a self-reliant mind-set—an attitude that you can rely on yourself to protect your family and property during any emergency, including a major natural calamity—is the first key step. (Remember the little old lady high up on Moscow Mountain!) The second is to develop plans to handle any type of emergency that might hit, including the procurement of proper equipment and supplies.

Keep in mind that large numbers of people happily choose to live in the country despite the potential for natural disasters to strike. As a general rule, folks who enjoy rural life accept and deal with whatever calamities may befall them. Those who don't soon retreat back to the cocoon of big-city life.

Chapter Nineteen

Down on the Farm

After my experience living on a farm, I know that the romantic myth of the family farm is, in fact, a romantic myth. Why anyone would push government programs to encourage and prolong such an awful institution is beyond me. Even farm veterans who are decades removed from the ordeal will, if they are honest, quickly recall the poverty, the dirty, difficult, long hours, and the uncertainty, discouragement, and danger associated with life on a family farm. Just as soon as a job opened in town, we took it—anything to have a steady paycheck and not have to work so hard out in the dust, mud, manure, and snow.

This is not to say there is no uniquely enjoyable rural culture, only that it may not be the romantic ideal many city slickers envision. Latest statistics indicate that just over 3 million Americans still make their living on farms. (This does not count farm-related employment from such support industries as food processors, farm equipment manufacturers, and so forth.) Very, very few of these are actually small family farmers. (I'm not talking about mammoth farms run by a single wealthy family, nor those operated by agricultural conglomerates like ConAgra.) Most of your neighbors will probably be long-term rural residents who work in town but live in the country. Like me, they may have a farming background, but they will no longer make their keep that way. But there will still be farmers and ranchers out there—some small, some large; some full-time, some part-time—and learning to live side-by-side with them and their ways is what this chapter is all about.

Until Mark Sillman woke up one morning to find a herd of cows in his yard, he thought "open range" referred to leaving the kitchen stove door ajar.

There they were in all their glory, milling around contentedly, scarring his lawn, eating his bushes, and destroying his delicate mountainside terraces. Sillman's 100 percent organic garden was a shambles—beaten, eaten, trampled, and covered with fresh, 100 percent organic cow droppings.

Open range, Mr. Sillman discovered to his dismay, means that it is your responsibility to fence livestock out rather than farmers and ranchers having to fence their critters in. City transplant that he was, discovering that these cattle were legal trespassers came as a rude shock to Mr. Sillman, especially given the high levels of damage they brought with them.

The concept of open range in the American West is far from universal these days, but it is still sufficiently common that new rural property owners in livestock areas had best inquire. And the general issue isn't limited to domestic beasts. In the South it can be free-roaming wild pigs that homeowners must fence against. Feral goats can be a problem in parts of California, and in some areas of Idaho, Montana, and the Southwest there are still herds of super destructive wild horses and burros. Neglect this reality and you'll end up like Mr. Sillman, building expensive fencing after the damage has been done.

You will also encounter free-ranging animals on public lands in rural America. I won't saddle you with the history of rangeland and grazing in the United States, but the fact is, livestock still have a wide berth to graze on public lands in this country. Ranching communities will always side with the cowboys working their cattle over the hiker or biker blocked on the trail who doesn't know how to move through or around the beasts. Same with a pile of cows or sheep being driven down the middle of a public road, blocking your path and making you late for your chiropractic appointment. If you disturb the animals out of ignorance or spite, you will most likely be on the receiving end of a tongue lashing or worse by the guys or gals in charge of the herd.

Farm animals are not only a nuisance, they can be dangerous. I can recall at least five local incidents where city slickers were hurt by farm animals. Two involved randy dairy bulls, two involved difficult stallions, and one involved curious hogs. Farmers can sometimes be held liable for dangerous male breeding animals that can get uppity at times, but some responsibility should reside with neophyte rural transplants when they encounter these critters.

The infallible rule here is that farm animals are not pets, nor are they especially docile. It is extremely difficult to get rural newcomers to understand this simple fact. Forget about the cherished trips in your youth to "Olde MacDonald's Farm" petting zoo. Farm animals are animals, which means they can be unpredictable. If you are out jogging and encounter a large male farm animal or a mama with her young, give them a very, very wide berth or turn around and continue your exercise in the direction you came. You'll have plenty of other opportunities to jog that route in the future.

Another classic example of this culture clash over livestock occurs when some recent transplant from the city allows his dog to run free on their property. We're out in the country now, right? The dog can romp and play to his heart's content off leash, right?

Wrong. Countless times, these dogs burst onto a neighboring farmer's land and chase and sometimes kill chickens, sheep, cattle, and horses. How does the farmer respond? He gets his shotgun or varmint rifle out and shoots the dog dead. The enraged dog owner, weeping kids in tow, races down to the sheriff's office and demands justice. Sheriff just shakes his head and informs the sputtering newcomer that *he* was in fact in violation of the law and the livestock owner had every right to protect his property with force. Many recipients of this form of frontier justice end up packing up and heading back to the city, mystified about the seeming barbarity of this reality of life in the country. Others accept the lesson learned and mind their pets carefully from then on.

Here's another common culture clash in the country. A lady living near Boise, Idaho, complained bitterly about odors from a cattle feedlot. Her new home was situated 500 yards from the cows and their mountain of refuse, but winds were often not to her advantage. Chicken and hog factories can stink equally bad. Farmers tend to think this smells like money and do not take much note of either odors or complaints.

Some simple agricultural practices, when implemented, can reduce farm odors. Problem is that stockmen do not tend to implement these practices on behalf of testy city folks who voluntarily moved into their neighborhood. That was the case here: the lady near Boise quickly came to the opinion that city air was purer than country air and moved back to Seattle.

If there is a golden rule of living peacefully next to farmers or other rural neighbors, it is to talk with them now and then. Don't waste their time during planting or harvest or other critical times, but sometime soon after moving into the area, stop and chat with your new neighbors.

What to talk to your farmer-neighbors about? Three subjects virtually guarantee a full afternoon of conversation: the weather, low farm commodity prices, or the grandkids. Do 15 minutes of this now and then and you will have no problems. Your friendly farmer may even start to loan you tools, plow your lane, or ride your kids to the school bus.

Just remember that farmers block absolutely everything else out of their lives till their harvest is safely gathered in. Once harvest actually starts, farmers fret and stew about weather anomalies, equipment breakdowns, or anything else that might hinder their work or degrade their product. As a result, they may labor from well before dawn till well after sunset at harvest time. This provides another lesson about life in the country.

Non-farming property surrounded by harvesting fields may be subjected to continuous noise from heavy machinery, shouts from field hands, and tractor lights through bedroom windows. This may go on for several days or weeks until harvest is completed in that field.

In the case of hay operations, some farmers work at night rather than in the heat of the day. This is an attempt to keep frail alfalfa leaves from shattering away from hay stems by handling the plants at night when they are a bit damp. Loss of these valuable leaves to dry daytime conditions significantly degrades the quality of their crop. The cost in dollars lost can be significant. It's not an intuitive situation for non-ag neighbors, and it's not something you can find out easily without talking to your friendly local farmer. Just don't try to talk while he is trying to bale hay!

Farmers don't enjoy working 'round the clock or late night hours any more than average rural homeowners like hearing them work at such times. Like using pesticides and soil amendments, it's just the nature of the business.

Here's another common issue with transplants to the city: what to do about painfully slow-moving tractors or combines on your rural road?

The solution is simple: switch on the emergency blinkers, slow to 15 mph, don't tailgate the driver, and help him or her (wives or daughters often help transport equipment) keep safe. Pass only when it's safe to do so, and do it slowly and with a wave. It's not a face-to-face talk, but it is very effective communication—that you are an accommodating, patient member of the community. Farmers don't like to be an encumbrance any more than they like to be encumbered themselves. Next time they will pull over to let you by just as soon as they safely and reasonably can do so.

Some farmers, especially in irrigated areas, burn weeds and stubble along lanes, ditch banks, and irrigation ditches. Smoke, smell, and haze from this burning sometimes irritates newcomers unused to the procedure. It also may alarm them, precipitating frantic phone calls to the fire department about wildfires sweeping the countryside. Imagine the embarrassment for the caller when he later learns that he mobilized a troop of firefighters to respond to a bewildered farmer and his smoldering patch of stubble.

A few older rural folks still use burn barrels for their household trash. Unlike burning overgrowth and weed patches, burn barrels are banned in many states and strictly controlled in others. Laws notwithstanding, old-school country dwellers continue to burn their trash in outside barrels illegally.

The issue of burning can become quite heated, so to speak. Rural transplants in eastern Washington and northern Idaho are currently battling with established farmers over field burning. Historically, farmers burned stubble from their bluegrass fields to clear them of weeds, kill any seeds not of the crop being planted, and shock the ground into higher production. Without fire, bluegrass quickly degenerates into seed yields of only a few pounds per acre.

Non-farmers despise the dense, choking smother created by the burning. Farmers point out that bluegrass is currently their only profitable crop, and that bluegrass seedlings are used to mitigate environmental damage and to improve water quality.

If forced by lawsuits to sell out and abandon their operations, the entire area will become a subdivided city, destroying all rural ambiance.

Stung by what often seems to be irrational criticism of normal, established agricultural practices, many states have enacted Freedom to Farm legislation. These laws heavily mitigate against city slickers, making it very, very difficult to change traditional rural practices.

Some change might occur, but it will take time. For example, complaints about stinking livestock operations have led to research into methods to dramatically reduce livestock odors. Our land grant colleges may come up with an answer yet, even if these changes tend not to be as fast or as sweeping as some city transplants wish.

Bottom line is that whatever you see, smell, and feel on and around your rural property is what you get. Learn to live with rural culture, because chances are you won't be able to change it.

Chapter Twenty

Rural Churches and Their Role in Local Affairs

In a surprising number of areas, local churches still play a major social role in rural society. It seems helpful, then, to briefly visit this issue in order to better understand the workings of rural communities.

In many rural communities, social, governmental, and economic activities organized within and around local churches are so important that, if there were no church umbrella structure to organize and coordinate, one would have to be invented. This role was served at one time by granges and fraternal orders like the Elks, Odd Fellows, and Masons, but these social groups are withering away as their memberships age and young people find other outlets for camaraderie and social service.

Before, during, and after Sunday morning meeting, farmers historically made their week's arrangements with their neighbors: see their fat hogs and cattle trucked to market; borrow or rent a bull or boar; hire a neighbor boy to clean the cattle stalls or a girl to clean the root cellar; let everyone know that 24D week killer will be sprayed in the following week and to cover their tomatoes; discuss county commissioners' decisions and agree on appropriate responses; announce engagements, deaths, and illnesses; lay plans to assist those in need; and hundreds of other chores, issues, and notices.

This list is nowhere near inclusive. It is hardly even representative. Virtually anything and everything was on the table for planning, coordination, and discussion among church attendees. Although this practice may not be as prevalent today, some degree of social, business, and political interaction is still a part of modern church life.

These days, membership in a specific church is usually not nearly so important as simply not being perceived as being antagonistic toward that church or churches in general. If you suspect a specific church or group of churches is an important socio-economic force in the community, you had best make peace with that group. If nothing else, use it as a tool to test the community pulse and accomplish objectives like getting help and advice when necessary.

I am often asked if rural preachers control or influence the thoughts and actions of their congregations. To a limited extent they might. But church policy is usually set by longstanding tradition, including concepts that generally reflect those of the entire region. Preachers who espouse principles outside conventional bounds are either ignored or asked to step back into acceptable parameters. If, however, you actively and overtly push concepts that run contrary to the congregation's general mores and outlooks, you should naturally expect some bristly reactions.

Even if you have no specific reason to do so, if a church is within a mile or two of your new rural paradise, stop by one Sunday morning to visit and attend services. After service, linger and talk with your neighbors and any new friends you may have. In the unlikely event they press for membership, tell them you are church shopping. There are exceptions in some hard-core communities, but questions about your faith or urgings to join will generally not come up. If ever questioned or confronted by overly zealous parishioners, just use common sense and diplomacy and you will be fine.

Does the thought of going to church to meet your neighbors, learn what's going on in the community, and organize projects really turn you off? There is almost as good an alternative!

In many rural communities, church and Wednesday night prayer meeting attendees gather for lunch or pie and coffee at a local restaurant after services. Discover which restaurant and show up for this informal get-together. Most folks will assume you attend services, but at another fellowship. They will enter into their regular organizational, community gossip, and report pattern with you at the restaurant.

Wise transplants who aspire to an easier, more comfortable, accommodating life out in the country had best at least consider the role of the local church in the community. Mainly, just don't appear antagonistic. Again, church membership is not nearly as important as being perceived as being a person who is not hostile toward church and the rural culture it represents.

Blending In

Blending seamlessly into your natural surroundings is part of the delight of your new life in the country. Unfortunately, many city people think of blending with nature but forget about social blending.

In this chapter, I will attempt to identify vague, difficult-to-articulate cultural aspects of rural life such as dress codes in the country, how to identify rural wealth, avoiding unnecessary antagonism from the locals, and other more mundane issues. In all cases, just remember that common sense and good manners will always serve you well. Yet by knowing about some of the social customs of the country beforehand, newcomers will have a better foundation upon which to apply their manners and sense during their interactions with new neighbors.

It is a cliché of country life that rural people are incorrigible gossips. Even though neighbors may see each other only occasionally on their respective rounds, long-time rural dwellers all seem to know each others' business, often in what outsiders believe is remarkable detail. This stereotype may be true to a degree, but it must be balanced with another: that people in the country have a live-and-let-live philosophy, meaning that as long as you don't interfere with their way of life, they won't care how you choose to live yours. The truth, as usual, is somewhere in the middle, but starting this chapter by exploring gossip and nosiness in the country provides some insights that may be useful to know.

Answering the question *why* rural folks can be busybodies at times really boils down to a couple of obvious factors, when you stop to think about it. Through all of this, keep in mind that this gossip is seldom meant to be mean or vindictive (although it can get that way if it involves a clash of personalities).

First, I believe rural folks poke into their neighbors' affairs because they can. Relatively speaking, there just aren't that many people out there. Doesn't take long to hear a thing or two about most everyone in the community. When local marriages are factored in, family and interfamily relations span great segments of the immediate population. Everybody seems related to everybody else. (Spare me the jokes, please.) Successful city transplants are eventually factored into the entire local network of information exchange.

Second, there is a strong element of boredom that contributes heavily to rural nosiness. In times past, country people were consigned to dull, repetitive lives. Following the horses and plow across the same field, dreary hour after dreary hour, was all there was to do for the man of the house. Modern farming brought tractors and other mechanization, but there were still hours of boredom running the machine end to end over a flat field. In the home, the wife canned beans, tomatoes, and peaches, and washing clothes by hand was about as intellectually stimulating. As a result, farmers could only talk about the weather, low crop prices, or—especially if there were no grandchildren yet—the neighbors.

Perhaps those concerned about local rural gossip can compare it to workplace gossip. I have no personal experience, but I understand that gossip can also run rampant within business organizations. Fellow workers talk about the those they know about or the high-profile guys and gals at the top. It's pretty much the same out in the country. Seems those who can endure one can endure the other.

Granted, some of this talk, talk, talk results from pure jealousy. Build a mansion on the land of a recently repossessed farm or move in with a fleet of shiny, new diesel pickups and it may be too much for some neighbors. Speculation will commence. Similarly, speaking down to local folks or telling them something is none of their business only intensifies their resolve to find out as much as possible.

How to minimize gossip? Perhaps the best advice is to recognize that rural gossip is not generally mean, nasty, and destructive and to simply live with it. Another remedy is simply to get to know your neighbor before rumors about you begin to fly like started barn pigeons. Make it a point to meet all the neighbors on your road within perhaps two miles. Most likely these visits will total no more than two, three, maybe four families. Don't just burst in on them, but maybe stop and introduce yourself if you see them at the mailbox, or have a plausible excuse to seek their advice about a fence line or wetland area.

As noted, the weather, low crop prices, or the grandkids are all safe topics, but do not talk about yourself exclusively. Instead, take an interest in their lifestyle. Deploy the "five Ws" approach from journalism and unobtrusively ask who, what, where, when, and why about them. Don't make it an interrogation; make it a sincere effort to get to know a little about the history and denizens of the community in which you have arrived.

You don't like the idea of visiting stinking farms and talking with dull, dumb farmers? You can get some of the same benefits by talking to store clerks, service providers, and other members of the community. In the meantime, just try to keep a low but non-secretive profile. Do not do anything particularly obvious or note-worthy, even if you think it will endear you to the locals.

Getting to know your neighbors, even casually, can pay dividends in times of crisis. Rural folks still pull together for the common good and help each other in times of distress. This is probably an artifact from traditional rural life back when farmers frequently banded together for large work projects or other mutual assistance. Today, somebody in the neighborhood has an accident, gets sick, or suffers a sudden calamity and neighbors rally to the aid of that person or family. The victims don't ask for government help, and the neighbors don't wait for it to arrive. They just pitch in without being asked.

Here is a real-life example. Happened to a friend living with his family in far western North Carolina in the mountains. He suffered horribly as the result of a grisly sawmill accident. Neighbors whom they scarcely knew and with whom they seldom spoke immediately came forward with great dishes of prepared food. People in the tiny crossroads village spontaneously donated money. Errands were run. The truck was fueled. It got to the point that the fellow's wife became embarrassed over so many strangers bearing gifts and help.

Some newcomers might not understand when a virtually unknown neighbor calls saying so-and-so was hurt falling off the roof and asks if you could please cook a meal, run some errands, or help provide temporary food and shelter for their children. Those put off by such an outpouring of compassion and aid had best reconsider living in the country, or look for a location where this tradition has faded.

One of the greatest social errors newly arrived city people make is assuming that established rural folks are poor because they look poor. Be sure to take note of the following information. It will be on the test.

There are no valid criteria or methods by which people new to the country can gauge other people's personal wealth. Even today, common city standards do not apply.

Wealth cannot be evaluated by the vehicle a neighbor drives. People who could easily afford a brand new, top-of-the-line luxury car frequently drive battered 10-year-old pickups.

Homes tend to be modest, even rustic. You'll find few, if any, expensive paintings, statues, figurines, sculptures, rugs, or other similarly costly, impractical bric-a-brac.

People for the most part dress modestly, without funky jewelry or baubles. Because of the danger of losing fingers in machinery, many rural men and women do not wear wedding rings. People who could afford Rolex watches often rely on cheap Casio models that, as they'll be happy to inform you, tell time just as well as the expensive brands.

Finally, it is difficult to determine if the family is stinking rich because of their employment. Much has been written already about small town businesspeople who have accumulated vast fortunes—usually in the most mundane, common sorts of enterprises—without abandoning their otherwise humble personal lifestyles. No flashy CEO positions or titles. No stock options. No glamorous enterprises and magazine profiles. Just hardworking people quietly running a successful business, raking in money, and spending it on sensible things and saving the rest.

In my own community, I think of the two brothers who had a tractor parts business, the fellow with the fabric store, and the guy who delivered coal for 40 years. Another gentleman came to town penniless but made his considerable fortune selling furniture. Probably the most graphic example is the Ph.D. chemical engineer who started a business filling computer printer cartridges. He became a multimillionaire in five years.

None of these folks wore their wealth on their sleeves or, for that matter, on their backs. Their kids attended local public schools, they usually remained married to their first wives, and they otherwise tended to live frugally but comfortably.

The bottom line is, just because a man or woman dresses plainly, works with smelly livestock, or putters in the dirt is no indication they couldn't write a $50,000 check for a breeding stallion that catches their eye. Until you know a bunch more about the financial situation of your neighbors, keep it low-key about your own.

City people sometimes ask us for advice about how to dress to fit into their adopted rural communities. They don't feel quite comfortable or genuine wearing what the locals wear, but they know that what they routinely wore in the city won't cut it out in the sticks. The advice is the same for men and women: dress in a manner similar to local branch bank managers, and dress your kids to the same standard of expense and style as his or her kids. Branch bank managers must get along with everyone in the community, so they will know what is appropriate for a person of their position.

A common mistake some people make is to move out from the 'burbs or big city and start dressing in a manner that they perceive to be proper country style. City transplants are often so pleased to leave urban customs, mores, and social patterns behind that they adopt rural patterns more intense than the natives. In some cases, affecting this new lifestyle becomes a virtual obsession. You'll see a new fellow in brand-new bib overalls or a long duster cowboy coat with a shiny Stetson perched on his head. If the clothes aren't dusty and battered, that's your first tip-off that he probably doesn't do anything more strenuous than pushing a button on his laptop to check on his stock portfolio. There's nothing wrong with donning jeans and a work shirt around town, but don't overdo it and pretend to be something your not with your choice of clothes.

Properly blending into a community also involves identifying and befriending key players. Some of these people are not obvious. Mention has already been made of the role that road grader and snowplow operators play in small communities, but they are only one set of people who have a major impact on quality of life in rural America.

How about the school bus driver? Most districts forbid their drivers from traveling or making pickups on private lanes. They have prescribed routes on regular rural roads from which they are not to deviate. In spite of this impediment, gregarious, friendly residents who know the system and have kids in school frequently cut private deals with bus drivers. These deals are centered on allowing the drivers access to your private road to provide him or her with a better, safer, easier place to pull over, turn around, or otherwise maneuver their lumbering yellow monsters. It's all wink-wink and really about having a more convenient pickup location for your children. Such deals can only be made when the school bus driver is a personal acquaintance.

Really remote rural residents usually pick up their mail in town once a week, once a month, or whatever. Most of the rest of us will have a carrier who places our mail in our rural box every day. Being on a personal, first-name basis with this person is vital.

In addition to delivering mail, rural carriers will keep an eye on homes when the owners are away on vacation or business, watch for important mail, and report suspicious vehicles, people, or activities in the area, and they are wonderful, fundamental sources of information about what's going on. Don't want to be the subject of gossip? Get to know your carrier personally. Convince that person you are average and reasonable and local gossip will fade like a snowbank in May.

While we're on the topic of mailboxes, here is another practical suggestion from yet another kibitzer. Rather than purchasing a cheap tin or plastic postal box in town, consider having a heavy 10 or 12 gauge steel box custom welded together. Local welding shops or a neighbor with the tools and skills can do this work. Mount this box on a heavy treated post set deep in the ground. Snowplows, road graders, vandals, and careless neighbors are unlikely to damage this style of box. It's more expensive, but problems in the long run are diminished. Meeting another local craftsman such as a welder has obvious merit, too.

Accomplished rural residents also make it a specific point to get to know their FedEx and UPS delivery people. Expect all sorts of customized service as a result. The UPS driver on our route checks our house and property when we are gone, stores our packages in his home when necessary, and, during the winter, provides an update on road conditions. Not an absolute essential for country living, but a little thing that makes life more pleasant.

Mention was made of the necessity of locating local water pump and septic system experts, but the services of other skilled craftsmen will eventually be necessary, too. Think automotive repair, welding and steel fabrication, stonemasonry, concrete and asphalt work, carpentry, roofing, even catering. High levels of personal skill, competence, and pride of workmanship are still found in rural areas. Shyster home repair artists have a difficult life in the land of gossip. Stick around long enough and you'll learn who the skilled, honest tradesmen are.

To find these people, inquire with neighbors, lumberyard or hardware store employees, folks at church, and other parents at your kids' school. Contact craftsmen as needed and ask them only three questions: Can you provide me with three or four locals for whom you have done similar work? How much will it cost? How soon can you start? Contact all the folks given as references and establish to your satisfaction that the person is an upstanding worker who completes work to spec, on time, and within budget.

Once hired, the work is completed to your satisfaction, and the craftsman is paid in full, you can count on having an expert on call for life. Workers in one area of expertise usually know of others with other skills. My carpenter, for instance, led me to an accomplished carpet layer and stonemason. Both are now established members of my network of professional contacts.

Establishing a pay scale for rural craftsmen can be tricky. Newcomers and perceived outsiders are frequently charged higher rates than the locals. Get used to it. I, for instance, just paid $5 per hour more—for work not quite as good—at a welding shop 60 miles from here than I would have paid if I was able to secure the services of my usual welder. (It was a quick turnaround, and he was booked solid.)

Talk about price with neighbors and references. Determine whether you're better off paying by the hour or in one agreed-upon lump sum. Whatever you do, don't muck up the local economy by offering a great deal over going rates. Expect to be asked to pay in cash at times. Rural craftsmen dislike taxes as much as anyone, and many work on the black (cash) economy. Some do not send bills; they expect immediate payment on completion of the job.

It is also common for homeowners to purchase all needed supplies independent of a contract or hourly price for labor. Be sure to settle this issue before work starts.

Garbage is another huge issue for rural America. A county commissioner once told me that garbage and dogs took up 80 percent of his time. As a general rule, expect tremendous amounts of snorting and clawing over garbage.

Sorting through all this mess would tax a person as wise as a tree full of owls. My recommendation, after living most of 50 years in the country, is to stay completely out of it, even if entails paying scandalous county garbage fees for absolutely minimal to no service. Forget the idea of starting your own dump on some far corner of your land—it's illegal.

In spite of forking out high fees for which we receive virtually nothing, we always haul our own garbage, without complaint or comment, to the local transfer station. By heavily triaging for organic material for the garden and paper for the stove, we have cut our trips to four per year.

Some recent rural transplants don't like the idea of hauling smelly, leaking garbage in their cars to a smelly, muddy transfer station. Maybe a neighbor will take your garbage along when he hauls his in exchange for some reciprocal favor, or maybe there is a pickup truck in your future. Either way, heed my advice on garbage. It's one of those rural peculiarities that you can't win on if you try to change it.

Activist attempts to force change on rural folks are universally resented and sometimes have painful fallout. You may be a hard-core greenie, vegetarian, pacifist, complete anti-chemical Buddhist—and that's fine. Just don't wear it on your sleeve or try to break your neighbor farmer's rice bowl by forcing him to be these things, too. Harmless nosiness aside, rural people generally don't care who you are or what you do so long as you are willing to extend the same courtesy to them. So, why, oh why, do some city newcomers insist on descending on an area they consider to be perfect and immediately start trying to change things to look like the city they just left? Established rural residents simply cannot understand this activist mentality.

Mary Martin, an anti-everything activist, made a run at a local farmer who was tilling fields surrounding her home. She didn't care for his use of chemicals to protect and enhance his crop, so she notified the fellow shortly before harvest that he could not bring his grain-bearing trucks across her property, as he'd always done in the past. If he couldn't get to his fields near her place, she apparently reasoned, he would have to give up farming there.

Fortunately, a third party interceded before serious damage to the farmer's livelihood was done. He diplomatically emphasized the fact that she was already something of a pariah locally. Should the farmer lose his crop, she would probably never be able to hire a plumber, carpenter, road grader, veterinarian, or anyone else ever again. With this new perspective, everybody soon agreed to do the sensible thing and get along.

Easements, both recorded and verbally traditional, can be huge issues. Although this is not the entire lesson of the Martin affair, it is a good time to remind everyone to look carefully into who is legally entitled to use your property and who is using it informally.

New owners may discover that local horse people, for instance, have been using trails through the back woodlot on their land for years. In spite of the fact that you, the new owner, may not tolerate this activity (fear of lawsuits if someone gets hurt is the usual reason), these recreational users may persist. It may come down to a nasty confrontation or legal battle that most folks do not need.

Perhaps horses are okay, but what about snowmobilers, cross country skiers, ATV operators, bird watchers, or hunters and fishermen? Reducing or stopping these practices altogether can be difficult, especially if it's been going on for a long time. Costly fences may be cut and no trespassing signs removed, destroying any legal basis for precluding entry. Community tranquility may be strained at times when newcomers really don't need it. Be dead sure the problem is really a problem before taking action.

Some activist situations are not black and white. I think of the city newcomer to a rural area who figured out that emergency fire and medical vehicles might take 45 minutes to arrive on the scene. Not acceptable when grandma has a bad heart. But rather than taking personal responsibility for trundling an ailing family member into the truck themselves for a quick trip to town or for fighting their own fire, newcomer activists may lobby for faster, better emergency equipment or more expensive standby personnel.

Established rural folks tend to view these efforts as costly and, for the most part, ineffective. It's quicker and easier to make a personal one-way trip than to increase everyone else's taxes. Farming and other traditional rural pursuits are not hugely profitable. Additional tax expense is seldom, if ever, greeted with enthusiasm by very many farmers, business owners, and long-time residents with a stake in the health of the community.

At times, shaking up a rural good-old-boy network has merit. But only in retrospect. Newcomers may give so much blood in the process they may never recover, or recovery may take years. Those who wait four to six years before taking on an activist role, or who do so unobtrusively, are much more likely to fit into their new rural community.

There's much more to blending into a rural community than what I've touched upon here, but it's a start. Driving rural roads correctly, talking to store owners, and helping a neighbor out of a ditch in the winter are more valuable in terms of community relations than holding an open house. As I said at the beginning of this chapter, plain old good manners and common sense will see you through most situations.

Conclusion

In most cases, rural folks have already swallowed the live toad on the issues covered in this book. They already know how to deal with problems associated with life in the country because they have already dealt with them—either personally or vicariously through the experiences of friends and neighbors. They just go about with their lives, rarely fussing about their property lines, soil composition, septic or water systems, county roads, estate mechanization, or whatever. When they do, it's when problems arise or for personal planning purposes. Once you become established in your new home and have had some time to gain experience with these matters and develop a network of local contacts for advice and assistance, you too will pay them mind only when you need to.

The more intangible rural protocols we have outlined—blending in, becoming self-sufficient, dealing with neighbors properly, avoiding no-win political controversies, enlisting support of county workers, driving protocols, and so forth—come with experience and plain old good manners and common sense. If that doesn't sound like a tall order for you, I think you will find that you are ideally suited for country life.

Perhaps the final test for city slickers and suburbanites contemplating their first move to the country should be to ask yourself if dealing with all these new and different issues would be interesting and entertaining. Would you enjoy the challenge and pride of being self-sufficient while simultaneously being a contributing member of the community? Would it be part of the charm of living in the country, or would it become drudgery? No other person can answer this question for you.

Also, be cautious of spousal pressures to go rural. Instances wherein one or the other—but not both—badly want a place in the country have become formulas for disaster. One may think that some sophisticated women can never adapt to rugged rural life, but it isn't always that way. A lady raised on an Iowa farm who moved to the country with her attorney husband comes to mind. She loves it; he tolerates it. He claims the added expenses for maintaining a country place discourage him. She says having a big garden and yard of her own more than makes up for the expense.

Although we have addressed many issues in this book, we cannot possibly cover them all. When it comes to the nuts and bolts of things like gardening, tractor care, road maintenance, and the many other common tasks of country life, there is an entire universe of books, magazines, and Web sites out there that will provide you with all the instruction you need to do any job and do it well. We have at least touched upon the major issues that a lifetime of personal observation has suggested new rural residents will face. Hopefully readers will adopt an inquisitive, ambitious, adventurous attitude that will kick into high gear, and that handling these red-flag issues will only add to their delight at living in the country.